## The United States and the Americas

Lester D. Langley, General Editor

*This series is dedicated to a broader understanding of the political, economic, and especially cultural forces and issues that have shaped the Western hemispheric experience— its governments and its peoples. Individual volumes assess relations between the United States and its neighbors to the south and north: Mexico, Central America, Cuba, the Dominican Republic, Haiti, Panama, Colombia, Venezuela, the Andean Republics (Peru, Ecuador, and Bolivia), Brazil, Uruguay and Paraguay, Argentina, Chile, and Canada.*

# The United States and the Americas

Panama and the United States

Michael L. Conniff

# Panama
# and the
# United States:
# The Forced
# Alliance

The University of Georgia Press
Athens and London

© 1992 by the University of Georgia Press
Athens, Georgia 30602

Set in 10 on 14 Palatino
The paper in this book meets the guidelines
for permanence and durability of the Committee on
Production Guidelines for Book Longevity of the
Council on Library Resources.

Printed in the United States of America

96   95   94   93   92   C   5   4   3   2   1

96   95   94   93   92   P   5   4   3   2   1

Library of Congress Cataloging in Publication Data

Conniff, Michael L.
    Panama and the United States : the forced
alliance / Michael L. Conniff.
        p.    cm. — (The United States and the Americas)
    Includes bibliographical references and index.
    ISBN 0-8203-1359-9 (alk. paper). — ISBN
0-8203-1360-2 (pbk. : alk. paper)
        1. United States—Foreign relations—Panama.
    2. Panama—Foreign relations—United States.
    I. Title.    II. Series.
    E183.8.P2C65   1992
    327.7307287—dc20                           91-7319
                                                   CIP

British Library Cataloging in Publication Data available

*To Jimmy Carter, who accomplished the goal of five U.S. and many Panamanian presidents*

# Contents

# Acknowledgments

For my education about U.S.-Panamanian relations, my earliest debt of gratitude is held by Professor Ernesto Castillero Pimentel of the University of Panama, whose 1966 course on U.S.-Panamanian relations revealed to me new points of view. Three other professors there—César Quintero, Camilo Pérez, and Beto Quiroz—showed me the powers of keen intelligence and fine exposition. My mentors in U.S. universities were John Wirth and John J. Johnson.

Many people have read parts or all of the various drafts of the book, for which I am grateful: Miguel Antonio Bernal, Jorge Conte Porras, Alfredo Castillero Calvo, James Howe, William J. Jorden, Graham Matthews, Brittmarie Janson Pérez, Noel Pugach, and two anonymous outside reviewers. Special thanks are due to Lester D. Langley, the general editor of this series, for his advice and support along the way. A number of other people have helped the project in different ways, including Celestino Arauz, Leslie Bethell, Willy Friar, the late Carlos Manuel Gasteazoro, Thomas Holloway, Richard Koster, Tom Leonard, John Major, David McCullough, Bonham Richardson, Carol Rios, Steve Ropp, Paul Ryan, Nelson Valdes, George Westerman, and the professionals at a number of libraries and archives. I also wish to thank the many persons who gave me interviews, most of whose names appear in the notes.

The Fulbright-Hayes program, the American Historical Association (Beveridge Award), the University of New Mexico Research Committee and History Department (on whose laptop I finished writing the manuscript), and the Tinker Foundation all contributed financially and in other ways to the completion of the book.

Finally, I appreciate the forebearance of my wife Janet and my sons Daniel and Andrew while I worked on the manuscript.

Panama and the United States

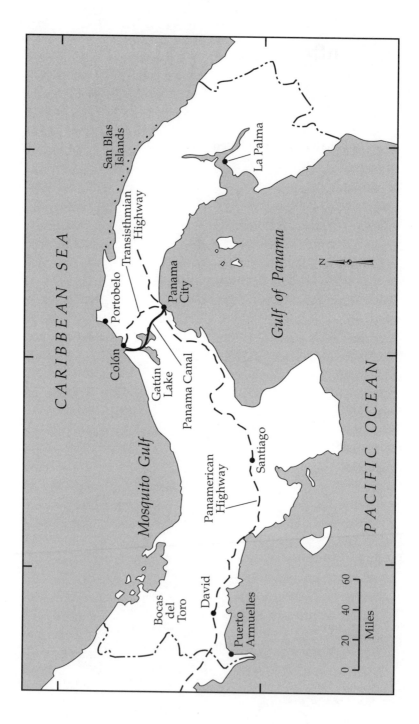

# Introduction

Since the era of Latin American independence, the governments and peoples of the United States and Panama have had fairly constant dealings with one another. These relations have not been as tempestuous as those between the United States and Mexico, Cuba, or Nicaragua, for example, but they have been troubled, at best, and unsatisfactory to large numbers of people in both countries. This book surveys U.S.-Panamanian relations over the past 170 years in an attempt to lay out the story succinctly and to offer interpretations of its most important episodes. It is cast as an authoritative reference work to be available to the general reader interested in how the United States and Panama have dealt with one another over the decades. I also hope that it will be used as a casebook or supplementary reading in courses on international relations. For the educated layman this book will provide background for better understanding problems that the two countries are experiencing in the 1990s.

*Panama and the United States* is set in the framework provided by Professor Lester D. Langley's *America and the Americas* (1989), the general introduction to the United States and the Americas series. This approach emphasizes a broad range of interactions between the countries involved, not just political and military but also cultural, economic, migrational, linguistic, and symbolic. In this view, an athletic contest or labor strike may be more significant than a president's speech or a foreign minister's correspondence. Perceptions that peoples have of one another and public opinion in general may play a larger role in international affairs than the professional conduct of diplomacy. And one need not be a Marxist to assign a preeminent role to economic factors in binational relations. This book portrays the mutual experiences of the United States and Panama in this broad fashion.

Beyond this innovative approach, I believe this book has other strengths that will make it valuable to the reader. First, it treats the actors as real human beings, whose behavior, dreams, fears, and personalities play important parts in the unfolding of history. I have described the Panamanians and the North Americans who led their nations' foreign affairs as honestly and understandably as possible. My acquaintance with some of these actors goes back to the mid-1960s, when I first lived and worked in Panama. Second, this book offers a long sweep of history in which isolated events can be seen from a longer perspective. Third, it draws to some extent on new documentation, interviews, and interpretation and goes beyond a mere synthesis of the secondary literature.

In the course of writing this book, I have stressed certain themes and subjects that are particularly crucial for understanding U.S.-Panamanian relations. Foremost is the notion of a forced and unequal alliance. The historical trajectories of Panama and the United States were destined to cross one another and to bond together. Panama has always aspired to become an international crossroads for commerce, travel, communication, and profit. The United States had long sought to create a maritime link between the Atlantic and the Pacific and to become the preeminent hemispheric and then world power. These two dreams began to merge with the U.S.-built Panama Railroad in the 1850s and became permanently joined in 1903, when the United States abetted Panama's independence in exchange for the right to build and operate a ship canal. The alliance is forced, however, in the sense that the two partners needed each other in order to fulfill basic national aspirations.

Once the alliance became embodied in the waterway and military bases in the former Canal Zone, it was forced in another sense too: the United States used its enormous power and wealth to impose its will upon the weaker partner. The Hay–Bunau-Varilla Treaty conceded canal rights "in perpetuity." The United States and Panama then played a classic game of great power–small power relations. Throughout this century, the colossus (as Panamanians sometimes refer to the United States) has used its tremendous influence to dictate policy to Panama. The latter has had to give in, retreat, stall, compromise, and protest since it had no forceful means of resisting such pressure. As a Panamanian diplomat wrote in 1927: "When you hit a rock with an egg, the egg breaks. Or when you hit an egg with a rock, the egg breaks. The United States is the rock. Panama is the egg. In either case, the egg breaks."[1] Thus the relationship has been unequal as well as forced.

The alliance is weakening and may dissolve altogether in 1999, when the United States turns over the canal to Panama. That was certainly the aim pursued by General Manuel Antonio Noriega, head of the Panamanian Defense Forces (PDF) and de facto ruler of the country between 1983 and the Christmas invasion of 1989. His stance seemed to be that the only way Panama could gain recognition as a nation was to fight against U.S. influences of all sorts. A man with few moral values but with a voracious appetite for power and wealth, Noriega became one of the most hated dictators of the region and for over two years withstood hemispheric demands that he resign. The U.S. position, meanwhile, held that the two countries must continue to work together with a modicum of dignity and mutual respect in order to fulfill the terms of the 1977 treaties. If the late-1980s crisis in U.S.-Panamanian affairs is any indication, the final decade of the treaties will be rocky indeed. Still, the concept of a mutually beneficial but unequal alliance from which neither can extricate itself without severe negative consequences must underlie any conception of the two countries' relations. Indeed, today's crisis is a symptom of impending divorce.

The U.S. alliance with Panama has lasted a century and a half, making it the longest in both countries' histories. Panama, moreover, always figured larger in Americans' consciousness than would be expected, given its diminutive territory and population. Policing the isthmus in the nineteenth century required the United States to maintain its first permanent overseas naval force, which became the Caribbean Squadron in the era of gunboat diplomacy. The United States gained its first military enclave in Latin America with the creation of the Canal Zone and its attendant military bases. The controversy over Panama's separation from Colombia and the task of building the canal commanded U.S. attention for over a decade. The 1977 treaties modifying the alliance caused the most heated treaty ratification battle ever fought in the United States. And the recent invasion constituted the largest U.S. military operation between the Vietnam War and the Middle East crisis of 1990. For better or worse, Panama has preoccupied the United States the way few other countries have. Arguably, Panama has received more consistent attention, money, and military protection from Washington than any other nation in the hemisphere.

Another important theme of this book is the way that constant immigration created new subcultures and made Panama a veritable melting pot. The Panama Railroad brought the first wave, the French Canal Company the second, and the U.S. canal project the third (but not last). These influxes, especially into the two terminal cities, altered Panamanian society and politics, created internal divisions, and destabilized governments. Negotiators for the two countries haggled endlessly over racial, ethnic, labor, citizenship, and migration questions. These conflicts and the real human changes they caused deeply affected U.S.-Panamanian relations. Even in the late 1980s, supporters of General Noriega against the United States referred to their opponents as the "rich whites" (*rabiblancos*). This book examines such sociological themes as well.

During the 1930s the United States began to experiment with economic aid as an adjunct to diplomacy, and after World War II financial levers of many different sorts were added to the statesman's tool chest. Economic matters became an important part of the relationship between the United States and Panama and will receive more attention in the final third of the book.

Public opinion played an unusually large role in the drama of U.S.-Panamanian relations because the railroad and canal satisfied major aspirations in both countries. Panamanians regarded these transit facilities to be essential for achieving their national destiny; Americans saw them as major elements of their country's geopolitical expansion. For Panamanians the canal in particular represented the nation's lifeblood; for Americans it symbolized the national genius. The military bases, too, evoked strong emotions. Panamanians saw them as violations of their sovereignty and foreign impositions; Americans regarded them as outposts of the free world. Therefore both Panamanians and Americans paid close attention to actions by their governments that affected the railroad, canal, and bases. Politicians disregarded public opinion on the Panama Canal at their own peril.

Ultimately, this book treats the experiences shared by Panamanians and Americans over a long period of time—not just diplomats but merchant seamen, businessmen, canal employees, foreign students, policemen, workers, union organizers, visiting scholars, housewives, touring performers, and countless other individuals. Their interactions are as important in this book as the formal discussions of diplomats and treaty deliberations. No amount of statesmanship can create good people-to-people relations, though it can certainly provide the setting for them. Likewise, if mutual respect and goodwill disappear from daily contacts, formal relations must deteriorate. I do not claim to have all the resources to tell such a story, but I include individual viewpoints to illustrate this facet.

This book ends on an unresolved note, a jarring harmonic situation, because of the impasse that exists between the United States and Panama in the early 1990s. Just as in 1904, the United States controls the isthmus militarily and politically, and a Panamanian president must submit major decisions for U.S. approval. This occupation reversed the trend, observable since the 1920s, toward greater exercise of power and autonomy by Panama's leaders in domestic matters. Such a historic reversal makes interpretation difficult and predictions especially risky. In the final analysis, though, I believe that future relations will be determined more by the attitudes of men and women in the street than by the rhetoric of political leaders. In this respect, we could perhaps rely more safely on evidence presented by Gallup and Roper than on the wisdom of Kennan and Kissinger. Regardless of whether this is a fortunate trend, it seems a fact of life. We will return to some of these central themes in the final pages of the book.

*Panama and the United States* has a straightforward structure for ease of consultation. Three-quarters of the text deals with the canal, the dominant topic in the two countries' relations, and one-quarter with its antecedents. The nine chapters correspond to chronological periods with fairly coherent events, actors, and outcomes. The more intense and dramatic the episodes, the more focused the narrative. I attempt to convey both countries' points of view (official and otherwise) as plausibly and fairly as I can. Toward the end the narrative becomes more reportorial and less interpretive due to the scant time and documentation available.

This book has some of the attributes of a historical novel: drama, strong characters, treachery, chance occurrences, intrigue, betrayal, violence, human suffering, and resolution. The two countries, somewhat artificially, are cast in the roles of protagonists—in fact, the story has dozens of protagonists, from Simón Bolívar to Teddy Roosevelt to Manuel Noriega. It has neither heroes nor villains, although the press cast some in those terms. Undoubtedly, the 1989 invasion constitutes the climax of the story, and the expected withdrawal and completion of the 1977 treaties represents the denouement. I hope that this drama will lead readers to watch the conclusion closely and help them to understand it.

This dramaturgical metaphor should not detract from the importance of the events narrated, for as suggested above they lay near the heart of the two countries' national aspirations. The main characters displayed dignity and courage, and the outcomes of their actions affected millions of people. The Panama Canal and the United States have always loomed huge in the lives of Panamanians, and the canal has likewise been a constant source of pride and concern to Americans. I certainly regard U.S.-Panamanian relations to be crucial for inter-American cooperation.

# 1    Independence and
Early Relations

In April 1819 the Scottish soldier-of-fortune Gregor Mac-Gregor and a ragged band of adventurers captured Portobelo, Panama's northern port for trade crossing to the Pacific Ocean. Acting loosely on behalf of independence forces in the Caribbean, he also enjoyed the backing of merchants in Jamaica, who desired freer access to the markets of Panama and the Pacific ports beyond the isthmus. MacGregor and his sponsors had a secret plan to build a canal if they succeeded in wresting Panama from Spanish control. The governor of Panama soon recaptured Portobelo and imprisoned MacGregor's men, so the scheme failed utterly.[1] This attack, one of three launched in the 1810s against the royalist stronghold, attested to the strategic importance of Panama in the tumultuous period of Spanish-American independence.

## Panama's Independence and U.S. Expansionism

Panama's leaders, late converts to the cause of independence, declared their separation from Spain in 1821. They annexed their land to the newly formed Confederation of Gran Colombia, a connection that would weaken as the century wore on. Prior to independence Panamanians had few dealings with citizens of the United States. Spain's loss of colonies in the hemisphere, however, brought a shift in U.S. policy, signaled by President Monroe's famous 1823 warning to the European powers not to recolonize former dependencies in the Americas. From then on U.S. leaders evinced a growing interest in an interoceanic crossing in Central America, especially at Nicaragua, Tehuantepec, or Panama. Panamanians, for their part, avidly sought

7

such a crossing in their province to restore commerce and spur economic development. By the late-1840s these two poles of attraction—U.S. and Panamanian aspirations—formed a connection and created scheduled interoceanic traffic across the isthmus. Such was the beginning of the U.S.-Panamanian alliance.

Panama had long served as a strategic locale in Spain's overseas empire, and her people had enjoyed special privileges in return. Until the eighteenth century virtually all Spain's trade with the west coast of South America had been transported across the isthmus. Her ports boasted modern fortifications, and her officials were paid well out of customshouse revenues and a generous subsidy (*sitiado*) from Lima. Panama was the seat of a captaincy and had a resident *audiencia*, or high court. Panamanians thought of themselves as destined to live by commerce and sought to have Spain establish a *consulado*, or board of trade, in their capital. Yet, since the 1730s, trade had slumped and the once-opulent fairs at Portobelo had virtually ended. The reasons were increased shipping around Cape Horn, greater commerce with non-Spanish vessels (that is, contraband), and the trade liberalization allowed after the 1770s. Spain's controlled, mercantilist system no longer benefited Panama.

Due to the drop in business, Panamanians increasingly embraced the doctrine of free trade in the eighteenth and early nineteenth century. Laissez-faire would become the dogma of the independence leaders and a panacea for later generations as well. This shift drew Panamanians toward the expanding commercial orbits of Great Britain and the United States.

Virtually no natural affinities existed between the United States and Panama prior to the latter's independence. The scant U.S. merchandise that landed at Panama in the 1790s and 1800s was usually handled by resident British merchants. Panama herself had little to sell to the world, and most U.S. trade at the time was with Europe, the Caribbean, and Brazil.[2]

Panama remained loyal to Spain during the 1810s. The struggles that broke out in the Spanish colonies after Napoleon's occupation of Madrid in 1808 did not cause immediate hardships in Panama nor did they provoke declarations of independence. The resident governor declared Panama's ports open to ships of friendly and neutral nations, causing a sharp increase in trade for the next several years. Many Panamanians sought to help the metropolis preserve its overseas empire. In 1810, for example, Panamanian soldiers joined military units dispatched to Quito and Bogotá, where patriot forces had declared their independence. Two years later the viceregal government of New Granada (modern Colombia) itself was installed in Panama due to a patriot rising in Bogotá.[3] The viceroy remained in Panama for a year and a half. Reinforcing the Panamanians' undoubted loyalty, however, was the realization that they would be fully exposed to Spain's naval forces should they attempt to rebel.

The restoration of Spanish control in New Granada and elsewhere in 1813 and 1814 and the relaxation of the emergency caused officials to restrict trade at Panama. In particular, powerful merchants in Cádiz objected to the transshipment of British goods to South America via Jamaica and Panama, which had been allowed during the crisis. The ensuing recession in Panama led to some of the first writings in favor of independence. In 1815, however, a new governor (authorized by the crown) again permitted merchants to trade with Jamaica, at that time the primary emporium for British goods in the Caribbean as well as Panama's natural trade partner. Still, authorities closed down the smuggling port of Chagres on the river of that name. These events strengthened Panama's ties to Spain in the turbulent 1810s but demonstrated that access to trade was a major condition for their loyalty.

Bolívar's victory at Boyacá in August 1919 and Rafael Riego's revolt in January 1820 turned the tide of war in South America in favor of independence. Shortly afterward the governor of Panama died and was replaced with a liberal dedicated to constitutionalism, elections, and open politics. This short-lived permissiveness was soon countermanded by the viceroy of New Granada, who arrived in Panama pursued by Bolívar's armies. The viceroy—bent on raising money and troops to fight Bolívar—angered local citizens and probably spurred the independence movement in Panama. He too died within a few months and was replaced by a military officer who continued the campaign to beat back the patriot forces. In the course of 1821 most Panamanians, chafing under the exactions of military government and heavy taxes, shifted their loyalties to the cause of independence.[4]

The movement for independence in Panama crystallized in the out-lying town of Villa de los Santos, with the so-called Grito de la Villa of 10 November 1821. Soon two other western towns—Pesé and Natá—followed suit, and outbreaks occurred in Panama City itself. A con-spiracy developed in the capital, at which point the small army unit abandoned its garrison. On 28 November leading citizens of Panama convoked a *cabildo abierto*, at which they declared their independence and annexation to Bolívar's Confederation of Gran Colombia. Thirty-one persons, among them Panama City's leading landowners and merchants, signed the act. No blood was shed.[5]

The new government moved quickly to protect the interests of Panama's elite. One of its first acts was a commercial regulation, which authorized Panama, Portobelo, and Chagres to trade freely with ships of friendly and neutral nations. It established rules for arrival and handling of cargo and sought to suppress contraband. Gran Colom-bia received preferential status, for her citizens paid only 20 percent duties on goods imported into Panama. Chilean, Peruvian, Argen-tine, and Mexican traders paid 22 percent and all others 24 percent.[6] This short-lived law revealed the Panamanians' desires to promote free trade and to foster closer relations with former Spanish colonies.

Bolívar had great designs for Panama. When in January 1822 he learned of Panama's break from Spain, he dispatched an aide, General José de Fábrega, to accept the province's adherence to Gran Colom-bia and to establish a government there. Fábrega soon mobilized a military force to join Bolívar in Peru, and Panamanian soldiers par-ticipated in the liberation of that region. Indeed, Panama provided a strategic base for ferrying men and arms between theaters, much as it had served the Spanish before 1821. More importantly, Bolívar laid plans for a hemispheric congress to be held in Panama City, a site he believed might become the capital of a larger confederation of former Spanish colonies. Finally, Bolívar envisioned construction of a railroad across the isthmus to link the two seas.

Meanwhile, the United States, which had remained largely neutral in the struggles for independence in Latin America, now decided to recognize those new nations that had thrown off Spanish rule. President Monroe asked Congress in March 1822 to appropriate funds to support legations, long before the European powers were ready to extend recognition to the new countries. Monroe and his secretary of state, John Quincy Adams, hoped to convince their European counterparts that the time had come to end the warfare and allow the former colonies to rebuild themselves in peace. U.S. opinion favored recognition despite a lack of good information about the countries and peoples to the south.[7]

Colombia was the first Latin American nation to be recognized by any power, when Monroe and Adams accepted the credentials of Bolívar's chargé in Washington in June 1822. Indirectly, then, the United States also recognized the independence of Panama. Over the next two years the United States extended recognition to Mexico, Argentina, Chile, Peru, the Central America Confederation, and Brazil.

In 1824 Gran Colombia and the United States ratified the Anderson-Gual Treaty, the commercial clauses of which gave the United States most-favored-nation status. Several months later, however, the British managed to sign an even more advantageous treaty with Colombia, permitting their merchant vessels to trade in Colombian ports under the same rules as Colombian ships. As Eduardo Lemaitre notes, this undermined attempts by the young nation to develop its own merchant marine.[8] U.S. shippers carried on little trade with Colombia in those years.

From the mid-1820s on, Panama had a tumultuous political existence under Gran Colombian governance. Out of this experience arose a spirit of autonomy and a series of secessionist revolts. As the decades passed, Panama drifted away from Colombia. Also, imperceptibly at first, but then more clearly in the 1840s, the U.S. government took an interest in Panama as a site for an interoceanic crossing. Thus, at an early point, autonomy and development of a transit facility became linked in the minds of Panamanians.

Bolívar's congress, convened in Panama City in June and July 1826, would have been an ideal forum for the U.S. government to pursue its interest in the isthmian route, yet it was not to be. The congress itself proved a disappointment. Bolívar had already become a figure of great controversy, so he did not attend the congress. Chile and Argentina did not send representatives because their leaders suspected that Bolívar wished to control all of South America, and Brazil was only invited as an afterthought. Britain, the Netherlands, and the United States were invited as observers, and the former two did send delegates. The U.S. Congress, however, held up funds for Adams's emissaries until the last minute to express its members' independence from the president, who strongly favored attendance. Then one delegate died en route to Panama, and the other did not even embark.[9]

Secretary of State Henry Clay did, however, give instructions to his envoys to Panama, which included a policy on a possible interoceanic canal. The United States, he wrote, preferred that any such facility be built, operated, and protected jointly by the United States and other maritime powers. The U.S. goal at this time was principally free trade in the region. This internationalist approach, actually born of national weakness, would constitute the Central American canal policy of the United States for the next four decades.[10]

At about the time of the Panama congress, Bolívar's constitution for Bolivia began to provoke secessionist sentiment among Panamanians. The charter proclaimed the Liberator president-for-life and concentrated dictatorial power in his hands. Bolívar and his supporters lobbied to have it promulgated throughout Gran Colombia. In Panama and elsewhere demonstrations erupted against such a system, and a growing number of persons opposed Bolívar himself. Many also objected to the actions of governors sent from Venezuela and Colombia, whose policies of taxation and military conscription weighed heavily on the local population. The situation deteriorated after the onset of economic recession in the late 1820s.[11]

Between 1828 and 1830 the Confederation of Gran Colombia fell apart, as the Liberator's grip on power slipped and his health failed. By the time of his death, many Panamanians believed that they should declare themselves an independent "Hanseatic state" dedicated to commerce and protected by one or more of the great powers. A large contingent of Panama City's prominent citizens gathered in late September 1830 to proclaim their secession from Colombia. Three times the number of persons signed their proclamation as had signed that of 1821, including many petty officials and military figures. Their reasons included the lack of natural ties to Bogotá and their desire for economic freedom.[12] The movement soon aborted, however.

The following year Panamanians again declared their independence from Colombia and remained self-governing for over a month.[13] Eventually, though, Colombian troops arrived and restored rule. Many more people had signed the 1831 proclamation, representing the cream of Panama's commercial elite. By now a virulent depression gripped the isthmus, and the abandonment of proposals to build an isthmian crossing heightened the sense of disappointment. Panamanian economic leaders dreamed of their cities becoming free ports in which merchants, laborers, ships, and money could circulate without hindrance. That vision, and the possibility of a ship canal, became a panacea in the eyes of the Panamanians.

Meanwhile, the psychological distance between Panama and Bogotá increased, as did the spirit of autonomy in the former. Another independence movement occurred in 1840 and 1841, this time sparked by a bloody civil war in Colombia that hurt business on the isthmus. Sentiment in Panama was divided between those who favored permanent separation and others who preferred a temporary break with an eye toward attaining greater federal autonomy. Advocates of the former path went so far as to request recognition from the United States, but it was not forthcoming. When threatened with military action, the Panamanians returned to the Colombian fold.[14]

Those who regarded independence as impossible continued to campaign for more self-government and economic freedom within the Colombian federation. They were encouraged in the 1840s by the rise to power of the Liberals, whose program favored states' rights and free trade policies. Autonomist efforts, led by Panamanian statesman Justo Arosemena, culminated in the creation of the Federal State of Panama in 1855. Even then, however, disputes over self-rule and centralism versus federalism continued to disrupt relations between Panama City and Bogotá.[15]

## U.S. Expansionism

Once most of Latin America became free of Spanish control, foreign interest in a transportation route across Central America blossomed. Alexander Von Humboldt's famous *Political Essay on the Kingdom of New Spain* (London, 1811) and his other writings stimulated many proposals for developing such a route. Since three of Humboldt's nine canal sites lay in Panama, isthmian projects abounded.[16] French entrepreneurs proved the most active in the 1830s and 1840s, acquiring Colombian rights for building a railroad, a canal, or both in Panama. The British concentrated on routes farther to the west, in Nicaragua and Costa Rica, where they asserted protectorate rights over the farcical "Kingdom of the Mosquitos." They also had colonies in Belize and the Bay Islands.[17] The United States, though little concerned with Central America in those years, did dispatch a representative to Panama in 1835 to acquire rights for safe passage of American citizens and perhaps for development of a railroad or a canal. Four years later John L. Stephens went as a U.S. agent to survey possible routes in Central America.[18] None of these projects bore fruit, however, and only a few even produced topographical information about the various sites.[19]

The breakup of the Central American Confederation in 1839 and the apparent indifference of U.S. officials in the region led the British to resume their protectorate over Mosquitia.[20] The British aim was to avoid reunification and to consolidate their hold on Belize and the Mosquito Coast. At the same time, Britain planned to recognize the independence of Texas from Mexico, in order to deepen its presence and slow U.S. expansion to the south.[21]

From the late 1820s to the early 1840s, the United States had devoted little attention to events in Central America. U.S. trade with the region languished, due to a general depression and to the superior economic terms Britain had obtained in treaties. In addition, it was difficult to maintain regular diplomatic relations because of political turmoil and periodic wars. Instead, U.S. attention focused on other foreign areas, on exploration of the West and the Pacific Coast, and on events in Texas, which had seceded from Mexico in 1836.[22]

In the early 1840s, however, President John Tyler pursued a policy of territorial acquisition. Tyler sought to annex Texas and to reduce British influence in the region. American public opinion also stirred with an inchoate expansionism and anglophobia, fanned by increased British activity in the Americas. The 1844 election provided a clear choice on the issue, as Whig candidate Henry Clay (ambivalent on the question of expansionism) lost to James K. Polk, an outspoken advocate of Manifest Destiny and the settlement by force if necessary of territorial disputes with Mexico in the Southwest and with Great Britain in Oregon.[23]

Even before Polk was inaugurated, Congress passed a Texas annexation bill submitted by Tyler, and the latter signed it immediately. Polk assumed the presidency and commenced a vigorous diplomatic effort with both Mexico and Britain. Polk compromised on the Oregon question but not in the Southwest. He offered Mexico $25 million for the purchase of California and New Mexico and insisted that Mexico accept Texas statehood and a southern boundary at the Rio Grande. When that failed, he precipitated the Mexican-American War, using as pretext a skirmish between Mexican and U.S. troops in the disputed territory between the Nueces and Rio Grande rivers. In the course of the war, as the U.S. Army invaded central Mexico, there was a brief movement to annex all of Mexico. In the end, the peace treaty of Guadalupe Hidalgo (1848) provided for the cession of the Southwest to the United States. But wartime expansionist sentiment inspired several U.S. leaders to consider the annexation of Spanish Cuba and Mexico's Yucatán Peninsula.

The Mexican-American War, drawing on powerful expansionist forces in the United States, had a profound impact on America's international standing. The nation emerged from the war greatly strengthened, a power to be reckoned with in its new sphere. The annexation of northwestern Mexico gave the United States continental projection, and it was potentially able to assert itself in two oceans and against British Canada as well. The acquisition of Oregon and then California created the need for safe and rapid movement of people and mail between the East and West coasts. The discovery of gold in California in 1848 made the link indispensable.[24]

Just as significant for Central America, in 1848 Polk resurrected Monroe's congressional message of 1823, which warned the European powers not to intervene in the Americas, and he sanctified it as the Monroe Doctrine. While the immediate goal was to prevent the British from taking over the Yucatán Peninsula (where separatist elements had been seeking annexation to Britain, Spain, or the United States), the doctrine would become dogma in U.S. foreign policy for more than a century. In practice, the doctrine implied military action in the North American continent, henceforth the natural U.S. sphere of influence, to impede European colonization. This American possessiveness in the mid-1840s ran head-on against British actions and generated great friction over the next fifteen years.[25] The revival of the Monroe Doctrine coincided with American designs to build a land bridge for ships across the Isthmus of Tehuantepec. A number of factors defeated the project, not the least of which was Mexicans' hostility after the annexation of half of their territory at the close of the war.[26] At that point, then, attention shifted toward transit rights in Central America.

## Central American Diplomacy

Preparations for an interoceanic crossing in Central America formed part of a global transportation revolution emanating from Europe in the first half of the nineteenth century. Technological development during the age of industrialization led to new means of transportation and communication, such as canals, macadamized roads, railroads, telegraphy, international cables, streetcars, and steamships. Most of these innovations took place in Europe and the United States, but adventurous men also looked abroad for opportunities to profit from reducing the time and cost of travel. Before long, Europeans and

North Americans were actively building transport facilities all over the world.

One of these early innovators in Latin America was the Royal Mail Steam Packet Company, formed in 1839 to provide fast and regular service between England and the West Indies. The following year British investors organized the Pacific Navigation Company to connect England and the West Coast of South America. Both companies received government subsidies for carrying the mail, and soon they got support from the Royal Navy in order to develop military uses for steamships. The British also saw the strategic value of packet service to their overseas empire. In 1846 the Royal Mail extended its runs to the port of Chagres on Panama's north coast and organized a canoe and mule service across to Panama City, where mail and passengers could rendezvous with the Pacific Navigation Company's ships. This was the first regularly scheduled crossing, even though the isthmus had been used for this purpose since the 1510s.[27]

In 1845 the United States, in a competitive, expansionist mood, took measures similar to Britain's to institute regular steam mail service to various coastal cities. For several years the Post Office took bids for carrying the mail, and some lines became functional. In 1847, in the heat of the Mexican campaigns, Congress provided more mail subsidy funds to the Navy Department by means of the Warship Act. This act authorized multiyear contracts for mail service in exchange for the navy's rights to oversee shipbuilding, train its officers at sea, transport troops and matériel, and take over vessels for wartime service if the need arose.

The navy's more generous funding gave it an edge over the Post Office for pioneering steamship service. As John Haskell Kemble wrote: "The prime consideration in bringing government assistance to the opening of the Panama route was that of the development of a more adequate steam navy for the United States. . . . A secondary reason . . . was the opportunity offered for training naval officers in handling of steamships in a period when the regular Navy had few such ships on its lists." The Warship Act helped make the navy preeminent in Caribbean and Central American affairs for the next half century.[28]

The first subsidized steamship line, which linked eastern and gulf coast ports, was authorized in 1847 to add service to Panama in the hope that regular communication could be provided to the newly acquired Oregon territory. This line would thus enter into competition with the British service established at Panama the previous year. In the meantime, U.S. mail service from Panama up the west coast to Oregon was bid separately in 1847 and was soon taken over by the New York capitalist William H. Aspinwall. The latter would soon make his mark on Panama by organizing a group of investors to build the Panama Railroad.

The maneuvers and contracts involved in the late-1840s scramble for U.S. mail subsidies are too complicated to detail here. In summary, consortia of hardbitten businessmen with personal connections to government officials took millions of dollars from the U.S. Treasury to build and operate steamships along the two coasts and to join the lines at Panama. The operators were neither altruistic nor patriotic. Kemble describes one of them in these words: "A product of his age and of the terrible competitive nature of the steamship business, [he] showed a lack of principle, a ruthless individualism, and a cynical view of political corruption for selfish purposes which were matched by many of his contemporaries and competitors."[29] Operators fought viciously among themselves, showed little concern for the public interest, and took advantage of the war to channel defense monies into their businesses.

Thus by the end of 1848, after the annexation of California and New Mexico, and on the eve of the great gold rush to California, the various steamship companies had been chartered and capitalized, and enough ships had come off the stocks to provide regular service.

In the meantime, U.S. diplomats and businessmen had actively sought concessions and guarantees for crossing rights at various sites in Central America. The Colombian province of Panama looked very promising, especially after the accession of free-trade advocates to power in Bogotá. In 1846 the U.S. chargé there, Benjamin Bidlack, urged the foreign minister to rescind discriminatory tariffs on U.S. goods that had been in effect for years. The minister, Manuel María

Mallarino, went far beyond Bidlack's request by agreeing to unrestricted transit of U.S. passengers and cargo across the isthmus by whatever means existed, on the condition that the United States guarantee the availability of transit as well as Colombia's sovereignty over Panama. Bidlack jumped at the opportunity and signed a treaty with Mallarino in December 1846.[30]

The Colombian position had shifted sharply from previous years. Unlike the leaders who had dominated government in the 1830s, the administration of Tomás Cipriano Mosquera (1845–49) favored free trade and generous concessions to develop transportation facilities, in Panama and elsewhere.[31] Moreover, Colombians no longer viewed the British as friends due to their reassertion of protectorate rights over the Mosquito Coast and to their territorial pretensions in Bocas del Toro, Panama. To Mosquera and Mallarino, the concession of transit rights to the United States in exchange for sovereignty and defense would block British territorial pretensions. At the time, Colombian and U.S. negotiators expected other powers to sign similar treaties with Colombia, giving the arrangement a multilateral character. In fact no other country did so.[32]

The Mexican war and other pressing business delayed U.S. ratification of the Bidlack-Mallarino Treaty. Polk did, however, favor it as a means of fostering trade and investment in Panama and of moving toward an interoceanic railroad or canal under U.S. control. To the objection that it constituted a binding alliance with Colombia, Polk pointed out that other powers were expected to sign, so that U.S. responsibility would be limited. The Senate ratified the treaty in mid 1848, inaugurating the first phase of the U.S.-Panamanian alliance.[33]

The Bidlack-Mallarino Treaty, negotiated in a relatively innocent manner, deeply altered relationships in Central America and provided for a U.S. presence in Panama far beyond what its signatories intended. It committed the United States to a crossing at Panama because it gave the government the right to intervene militarily to protect whatever transit facilities existed, even those owned by a third party. The United States thus gained a strategic interest in Panama, one of the first outside its territory. Second, the intervention right would be exercised a total of thirteen times by 1902, during which U.S. troops landed on the isthmus for considerable periods.[34] This had the effect of pitting U.S. agents against the local population, as an occupying force, a relationship of natural enmity. Third, the Sovereignty Clause of the Bidlack-Mallarino Treaty implied that the United States would prevent Panamanians from seceding from Colombia, as they had attempted to do several times before 1846. In effect, the United States controlled an important aspect of the political destiny of the Panamanians. Fourth, the treaty converted Panama from an "isthmus of Jamaica into an isthmus of New York."[35] Fifth, once the United States became the guarantor of free transit and Colombian sovereignty in Panama, U.S. leaders viewed actions of other powers in the region as threats to U.S. security. And finally, this was the only alliance treaty the United States ratified in the nineteenth century. Thus this extraordinary treaty marked the beginning of an intimate though not always friendly alliance between Panama and the United States.

By the time the Bidlack-Mallarino Treaty was ratified, the United States had defeated Mexico and annexed the entire northwestern half of that country. Within months U.S. steamships were providing rapid, safe transport to Panama and then to California. The simultaneous discovery of gold in Sutter's Mill provoked a great rush of people and goods to California, glorifying the importance of the Panama route in American minds. These events strengthened U.S. desires to exercise control in the region and caused the British to revise their policies toward Central America.

In the late 1840s many U.S. diplomats and opinion makers increasingly opposed British influence in Central America, especially in Nicaragua, which possessed one of the most viable canal crossings. Since 1848 the so-called Mosquito King (backed by British forces) had occupied both banks of the San Juan River and claimed as his territory Lake Nicaragua, from which it flowed. In early 1849, Zachary Taylor, who succeeded Polk as president, instructed his secretary of state to protest British territorial claims in Nicaragua. Public opinion became further aroused by the British military occupation of Nicaragua's Tigre Island in 1849. The United States, invoking the Monroe Doctrine again, implied it would go to war to prevent further acquisition of British territory in Central America.[36]

The fact that U.S. emissaries concluded treaties that same year giving the United States exclusive transit privileges in exchange for recognition of Nicaragua's sovereignty over the San Juan region heightened the Anglo-American confrontation.[37] Elijah Hise signed one on behalf of Polk, providing for exclusive transit rights and fortifications in exchange for a U.S. guarantee of Nicaraguan territorial sovereignty. Soon Ephraim George Squier, sent by Taylor, concluded a less demanding treaty with Nicaragua. The United States was clearly scratching a line beyond which it would not allow the British to step.

In view of the growing pressure from the United States, the British foreign secretary sent Henry Lytton Bulwer to Washington to seek a compromise. The colonial office and other high officials had come to believe that Britain was overcommitted to far-flung colonies and should withdraw gracefully from some of the more marginal ones. In the Central American context, this meant pulling back from Mosquitia but protecting English settlers in Belize and the Bay Islands. Globally, Britain should concentrate more on Africa and Asia and avoid trouble with the United States, its leading trade partner. A war with the United States would be very costly, threaten British influence in the region, and jeopardize Canada and other British territories. Still, whatever withdrawal took place had to be gradual and voluntary in order to preserve British honor.[38]

Bulwer determined that U.S. opinion was most adamant about Britain's ability to thwart plans for a Nicaraguan canal and even block trade there by means of its Mosquitia Protectorate. American opposition to British colonization in Central America and Belize, by contrast, was relatively mild. Therefore, Bulwer proposed to Taylor and Secretary of State John Clayton that they sign a treaty agreeing to share responsibility for the construction and neutrality of any interoceanic facility that either might undertake in Central America. In this way they could avoid competition over a canal and obviate separate treaties with the Central American nations to untangle their overlapping territorial claims. This concession from the most powerful and wealthy nation in the world meant the United States would not be excluded from participation in a canal project. The British would also forego colonization and alliances in Central America.

The resultant Clayton-Bulwer Treaty proved one of the least satisfactory and most contentious ever entered into by the United States. Article 1 contained the core of the agreement. Both sides pledged to share in any ship canal project across Central America. They would refrain from fortifying the canal and from establishing colonies near it. Neither would enter into alliances with Central American governments that might violate the pledge of collaboration. Citizens of both countries would have full and equal access to the canal. The parties further agreed to apply these principles to any other utility, such as a highway or railroad. Finally, the treaty encompassed all of Central America except, as agreed separately, Belize and its Bay Island dependencies. The document was signed in April 1850.

As American leaders soon learned, this seemingly simple exchange was too good to be true. U.S. public opinion favored a canal, to be sure, but a growing number of people wanted it to be U.S. owned, operated, and defended. Even at the moment of its conception, the treaty was out of step with American aspirations. It ignored the Monroe Doctrine and established a balance of power when the public really wanted a sphere of influence. It potentially nullified the various transit rights treaties that had been signed in previous years, including those of Hise and Squier. As William Goetzmann writes, it was "a diplomatic defeat for the United States, and a stunning British victory."[39]

The stormy ratification debates and public uproar during the next decade largely focused on the extent to which the treaty obliged Britain to withdraw from Central America. The U.S. interpretation held that all British territories except Belize had to be evacuated, while the other side claimed that the treaty only prohibited the acquisition of new territories. The long and complex debate is not central to U.S.-Panamanian relations, except in that it promised British participation in any transit facility built in Panama. The United States later argued that Panama, as a Colombian province, was part of South America and hence outside the purview of the treaty. For the remainder of the century the United States mostly tried to ignore Clayton-Bulwer in its relations with Panama, rejecting occasional British protests. Eventually, however, the two abrogated the treaty to give the United States a clear right to build and fortify a canal in Panama.

In hindsight, the most important outcome of the Clayton-Bulwer Treaty was the British decision to recognize U.S. strategic interests in the region and accommodate U.S. expansion there. It probably prevented open conflict between the two nations in the region, but it also prolonged the British withdrawal. Finally, the episode served notice to U.S. officials that canal issues could evoke some of the most inflammatory public debates on international policy, precisely because domestic and foreign interests overlapped but did not coincide. Time and again, U.S. policymakers would find themselves outflanked on canal matters by chauvinistic opponents.[40]

# 2    The Railroad Era

Shots rang out across the Panama City waterfront and the smell of gunpowder hung in the sultry air. Dozens of Americans holed up in the Panama Railroad station imagined that they would not live to see another day. An argument over a slice of watermelon earlier in the day had provoked a riot in which dark-skinned Panamanians had attacked American travelers waiting to board a steamer for California. The incident, the so-called Watermelon War of 15 April 1856, showed that the prosperity everyone had expected in Panama after the completion of the Panama Railroad the year before had not trickled down to the workers, many of whom were left jobless by the modern new facilities. The riots could be seen as a harbinger of future troubles caused by unequal sharing of profits from Panama's international crossing. They were the first spat in the U.S.-Panamanian alliance.

## The Boom Years, 1848–1855

While the diplomats fought for position in Central American affairs, the discovery of gold in California produced an uncontrollable westward rush of people and supplies from the U.S. Atlantic seaboard that nearly inundated Panama. The timing could not have been more propitious for the holders of the mail contracts. The new steamships and docking facilities seemed made to order for the gold rush. For the next two decades hundreds of thousands of westward migrants embarked in eastern ports and paid extravagant fees to be taken to California. U.S.-Panamanian relations were forged during the gold rush.

Overnight the California traffic shifted Panama's trade from its traditional Europe–South America orientation to East Coast–West Coast vectors. It flooded Panama with U.S. citizens, merchandise, capital, and culture and drew in those of other nationalities too. It produced a huge demand for improved overland transport in Panama and supplied the profits to justify building the Panama Railroad. It attracted migrants from Panama's rural areas into the terminal cities in search of money and adventure. It deepened the Panamanians' belief that they would one day enjoy great prosperity because of their location on a major maritime route. One historian calls the coincidental gold rush across Panama and the consolidation of a laissez-faire regime in Bogotá "two revolutions in one."[1]

William Aspinwall, who had established the steamship mail service up the west coast from Panama to Oregon in 1848, was a respected New York businessman whose fortunes derived from commerce. Not simply a speculator, Aspinwall was a visionary who had invested in steamships because he believed in the inevitability of booming trade with the West Coast.[2] The annexation of California and the gold rush fully justified his vision. In 1848 he and some associates obtained an agreement from the Colombian government to take over a lapsed concession to a French firm to build a railroad in Panama. The following year they incorporated in New York as the Panama Railroad Company and began to raise capital after Congress failed to provide a subsidy. Finally, in May 1850, they concluded a contract with Bogotá regarding terms agreed to in 1848.

The railroad concession of 1848 was a decisive event in U.S.-Panamanian relations, because it established ground rules for the conduct of private business on the isthmus during the following decades. The company gained the exclusive right to build and operate a railroad, highway, or canal across Panama, along with complementary steamboat service if desired. The concession ran for forty-nine years, but Colombia had the option to buy out the company after twenty, thirty, or forty years, for the sums of $5 million, $4 million, or $2 million dollars, respectively. The company received without charge all public lands needed for operation of the railroad plus 250,000 acres of public land anywhere in the isthmus. The ports at either terminus of the railroad were to be free of trade restrictions. The railroad alone would set tolls for service but would pay 3 percent of its dividends to Colombia. This contract was very generous, but in view of the obstacles the company faced, it was probably fair. It also reflected terms offered to the French concessionaires (except a halving of the period from ninty-nine to forty-nine years) and to railroads in the United States. In the spirit of laissez faire, the railroad acquired the power to organize and operate an international transportation facility with virtually no control by either government.

By the time construction on the railroad began in 1850, the demands of gold seekers bound for California hampered work and drained off laborers. The East Coast steamers arrived every week or two at the mouth of the Chagres River, where they disengorged passengers. A U.S.-run town called Yankee Chagres sprang up on the right bank of the river, opposite the Panamanian settlement of Chagres. There travelers contracted with canoe operators for the thirty-odd-mile trip up the river to Cruces or Gorgona, depending upon the river's depth. Then they completed the trip to Panama City on foot or muleback. These activities employed a great many laborers, who were able to charge high fees. In addition, the hotels, saloons, restaurants, brothels, and shops of all sorts that sprang up to serve the travelers required even more employees. So, for the years the railroad was being built, 1850 to 1855, labor was scarce and wages high in Panama's transit zone. This boom, practically a dance of the millions, would be repeated on numerous occasions afterward.

The railroad imported workers to supplement the locals, giving rise to one of the most contentious issues in U.S.-Panamanian relations. Thousands of West Indians, Africans, Europeans, North Americans, and Chinese were contracted and given their passage to Panama. The West Indians, mostly Jamaicans, proved the steadiest workers, and their numbers reached about five thousand.[3] A contingent of a thousand Africans arrived in 1852, followed a year later by a thousand Chinese coolies. A fairly large number of Irish arrived also. The Chinese made a lasting impression because of their exotic looks and habits and because many committed suicide when deprived of opium by the railroad bosses. In all, thousands of workers were imported or arrived voluntarily in Panama during the 1850s, and the local population was nearly outnumbered by foreigners in the transit zone.

Educated Panamanians generally eschewed manual labor in the hope of being self-employed or finding higher-paying, higher-status service jobs. The elite accepted the need for imported laborers yet resented the fact that they had no control over the immigrants' nationalities and qualities. They also worried that the many imported workmen who remained in Panama, especially nonwhite and nonwestern peoples, would undermine the cohesiveness of the population. This concern, often bordering on xenophobia, would arise again in the twentieth century.

The construction strategy was to begin laying track on Manzanillo Island, the Caribbean railhead, and push south to the continental divide. As the rails advanced, the supervisors could stay in close contact with the work and import supplies at Manzanillo, which became a company town. The line followed the right bank of the Chagres to the village of Barbacoas, where it bridged the river and continued over the mountains and down toward Panama City. After a couple of years, gangs working out of Panama City began laying track north to meet the main line. The first railroad contractors to attempt the work gave up in about a year, after which the company assumed direct responsibility. Later, other contractors alternated with company-employed crews, depending upon the availability of labor, supervisors, money, and materials.

The Panama Railroad turned out to be one of the most expensive in the world to build, due to the region's location, topography, and climate. The investment was conservatively set at $8 million. Therefore each mile cost over $170,000 to build, and maintenance ran far more than any other road at the time. The work climate was also one of the unhealthiest because of endemic diseases, which took far more lives than did work accidents. Perhaps twelve thousand employees died, including at one point the entire technical staff.[4] As a result of the highly publicized mortality on the railroad project, Panama gained a lasting reputation as a tropical death trap.

Crime plagued Panama during the period of railroad construction
and became an explosive issue for U.S. and Panamanian authorities.
The region had always attracted pirates because of the silver transported and stored there by the Spanish. Now tens of thousands of
well-heeled foreigners traveled across the isthmus, and gold worth
millions of dollars was brought back from California each year. Bandits called *derienni* soon began attacking mule trains and made off
with great plunder, killing many travelers in the process. By 1851
the problem had grown to serious proportions and was scaring off
travelers.

The local police did not provide enough law enforcement to suit
the railroad managers, who decided to employ their own police. The
president of the railroad concluded a secret agreement with the provincial governor to allow the railroad to patrol the transit zone and
to enforce justice in any way he saw fit.[5] He had absolute jurisdiction over railroad customers and any Panamanians in the environs.
To head up the force, later known as the Isthmian Guard, the railroad recruited a notorious Indian fighter and former Texas Ranger,
Ran Runnels. When he arrived in 1852, Runnels posed as operator
of a mule transport service. In reality, he secretly organized a vigilante force of mostly U.S. residents and began keeping a roster of
bandits, criminals, and suspicious persons in Panama. Operating at
night, Runnels's vigilantes caught and killed persons thought to be
outlaws. Twice they rounded up dozens of men and hanged them
along the seawall in Panama City, a grisly warning to anyone con-
sidering breaking the law. Runnels gained fame as the hangman of
Panama and became a legend in the American community.

Runnels did more than execute criminals. He also broke up a crude
attempt by a local Panamanian official to organize railroad workers.
He disarmed the police in a little town along the line, seized and
flogged the official, and threatened him (and anyone else) with death
if he tried to organize the workers again.[6]

The Panama Railroad, then, assumed almost complete governmen-
tal authority over the transit route, known locally as the Yankee strip.
Colombian and Panamanian officials, who were outgunned and in-

timidated, deferred to the foreigners. Once the railroad was completed, it became easier to patrol, so the Isthmian Guard was disbanded and replaced by a railroad security force. Local police again enforced the law in the terminal cities. Even afterward, however, U.S. naval forces would be landed from time to time to handle major disturbances. This shared police jurisdiction would create conflicts, sometimes armed, between the governments of the two countries for the better part of a century.

In late 1851 California-bound passengers began paying to ride the railroad as far out as it went, about ten miles, to avoid battling the river current. The company charged exorbitant fees that the victims of gold fever readily paid. As the line progressed, it threw more and more canoe operators out of business, until it finally replaced them altogether. The company earned over $1 million from these partial trips, which helped to keep work going and enabled the company to sell more stock on the New York market. More important, steamships began landing at Manzanillo Island (soon renamed Aspinwall) so that their passengers could ride the train partway across the isthmus. The railroad built a permanent pier and hotel facilities, and soon Yankee Chagres atrophied. Eventually, then, everyone who did business in the Caribbean port depended upon the railroad, and Aspinwall (modern Colón) became a company town.[7]

In the early days of the gold rush, a few enterprising North Americans began publishing an English-language newspaper, the *Panama Star*. It soon merged with another U.S. venture, the *Herald*, to become the *Panama Star and Herald*, owned by A. B. Boyd, a U.S. citizen. This newspaper became the independent voice of the American community in Panama, though it remained on good terms with the railroad. Since it served the affluent foreign community, it became the leading purveyor of business and international news on the isthmus.[8]

Increasingly, the entire transit zone came under the ownership and control of the Americans and other foreigners, which also implied an overpowering cultural influence. The dollar replaced the peso as medium of exchange, and English became as common as Spanish.

While foreigners reaped great profits from the California trade in the 1850s, Panamanians concentrated on service employment or real estate rents. High wages and plenty of imported goods created a dance-of-the-millions climate among workers, who by most accounts spent their earnings in bars, brothels, and gambling dens. Panama City grew from five thousand to thirteen thousand inhabitants between 1842 and 1864. Local families that owned land saw property values skyrocket in a few years. Some opened hotels and other businesses, but primarily for the Panamanians who swelled the city. By and large, foreigners preferred to patronize their own countrymen's establishments. The elite profited mostly from rents and land speculation.[9]

## The Heyday of the Panama Railroad, 1855–1869

The completion of the railroad in 1855 brought dramatic changes to Panama and sharply altered its relationship with the United States. First, the construction crews were replaced with smaller gangs, who continued to improve the line until 1859. Second, coast-to-coast passage on the train eliminated business in intermediate towns, and many of their inhabitants migrated to the terminal cities to look for work. Third, mule drovers and tenders were thrown out of work, as were members of the Isthmian Guard paid to protect them. Finally, the construction of a permanent pier in Panama City and inauguration of steam launch service by the railroad in 1856 left thousands of dock hands and boatmen unemployed. The Panamanian workmen had not foreseen the end of the labor boom and suffered greatly when the railroad was finished.

The foreign community in Panama continued to prosper, however, for its businesses catered to passengers in transit, usually several thousand people. The Panamanian elite also escaped the recession since their assets were secure in real estate. So the costs of readjustment fell largely on the working class.

Despite these local hardships, the railroad entered into a golden age of windfall revenues with the inauguration of through service.

Between 1855 and 1869, when the transcontinental railroad was completed across the United States, the company enjoyed the highest profits of any line in the world, paying off its initial investment many times over. Joseph L. Schott termed the line the "newest and largest land pirate on the Isthmus" because of its monopolistic rate policies.[10] The directors wished to concentrate on passenger service and bullion shipments and maintained tonnage rates so high that most bulky cargo continued to be carried around Cape Horn. In addition, the company transported U.S. mail for $100,000 per year.

In 1867 the Colombian government considered exercising its option to buy the Panama Railroad the following year for $5 million dollars. It could then be sold at a huge profit to a British firm interested in taking it over. In the end, the company managed to negotiate a new and far less advantageous contract to avoid a takeover. The new period was ninety-nine years, during which the railroad had to carry Colombian mail and officials free; improve the harbors in the terminal cities; and pay $1 million and annuities of $250,000 henceforth, in addition to the 3 percent of dividends. Colombia also reclaimed the right to build or let a concession for a canal. Despite these changes and the competition of the transcontinental railroad, the Panama Railroad continued to make respectable profits.[11]

Until the inauguration of the Panama Railroad, a Nicaraguan crossing operated by shipping magnate Cornelius Vanderbilt gave stiff competition to its southeastern neighbor. It is important to remember that throughout the history of U.S.-Panamanian relations, Nicaragua offered an alternative to the transit facilities in Panama. This set up a bargaining situation in which the United States could threaten to build elsewhere, and Panamanians faced the prospect of losing what they regarded as their geographical destiny. Gerstle Mack concluded that a canal in Nicaragua would have been nearly as serviceable as the Panama Canal, a conclusion we can extend also to the railroad, so this was not always an empty threat.[12]

Proposals for a canal or railroad across Nicaragua were almost as old as those for Panama, and indeed the year after Aspinwall received his concession in Panama, U.S. envoys signed two treaties for a crossing in Nicaragua. That increased the U.S. pressure on Britain to withdraw from Central America and led to the Clayton-Bulwer Treaty. Vanderbilt took up the Nicaraguan option in 1849 in an attempt to link his steamship line through to California. His Nicaraguan transit company, which began operations in 1851, consisted of steamboat runs up the San Juan River and across Lake Nicaragua, coupled with a twelve-mile mule or stagecoach trip down the Pacific slope to a pier he constructed at San Juan del Sur.

For several years Vanderbilt's transit company prospered, in part because of a publicity campaign he ran emphasizing the dangers of the Panama route. Because he had few heavy investments to finance, Vanderbilt could offer cut-rate passage, and his service helped drive down prices the Panama operators could charge. At its height in 1853 the Nicaragua route handled about a third of the outbound passengers and half of the returning ones. Fierce competition between these crossings and their associated steamship lines characterized the years 1850 to 1855 as giants of the business world fought for control of the new maritime route.[13]

When the Panama Railroad was finished, Vanderbilt realized, he would no longer be able to compete. After 1855, transits across Nicaragua fell to a trickle, so he began to buy up shares in the rival line. During the late 1850s his steamships took so large a share of the traffic to Panama that the original line paid him fees to stay out of the market. In 1859 Vanderbilt managed to get the mail contract to the West Coast, a subsidy that helped him to force a compromise on his competitor and to reestablish monopolistic pricing.[14]

The Nicaragua route continued to have its partisans for the remainder of the century, however. Southern congressmen preferred it because of its greater proximity to their ports, and they regarded the Panama mail subsidy as a sop to New York financial interests. During the 1880s French canal project in Panama, U.S. citizens kept open the option of digging in Nicaragua. The final choice of a canal route would not be made until 1902, and even afterward the Nicaraguan alternative was used to gain leverage over Panama.

## Impact of the Railroad on
## U.S.-Panamanian Relations

Panama became a protectorate of the U.S. government after the completion of the railroad, a role that often irritated Panamanians and violated the terms of the Clayton-Bulwer Treaty. For financial and other reasons, the Colombian government tended to leave peacekeeping responsibilities to the railroad and U.S. authorities. The railroad handled day-to-day security problems with its own staff, but on occasion it would call upon consular officials to bring in the U.S. military, under the terms of the Bidlack-Mallarino Treaty. When such an occasion arose, one or more naval vessels would anchor in Panama's main harbors, with troops ready to land if necessary. Fourteen major interventions by U.S. forces occurred prior to Panama's independence from Colombia (see table).

Despite lacunae in the data and varying definitions, we can make some generalizations about the extent of U.S. armed intervention in Panama during the second half of the nineteenth century. One author, probably counting only occupations of Panama City, estimated that U.S. military forces spent a total of 134 days ashore.[15] Our tabulation, covering Colón and Bocas, runs to about two hundred. By either count, this was the longest aggregate time U.S. troops spent on foreign soil in that period, except during the occupation of Cuba from 1898 to 1902. Second, the number of troops and length of stay tended to increase, peaking in the years 1901 to 1903. Third, the motive for intervention increasingly became fear of damage to the Panama Railroad during civil wars. Finally, even without troop landings, U.S. military presence in Panama was virtually continual, due to regular visits there by naval forces.

The British government objected to the U.S. protectorate in Panama, arguing that under the terms of Clayton-Bulwer such responsibility should be shared equally by the two powers. In 1857 Britain proposed a tripartite agreement for including France in protecting the neutrality of the Panama Railroad. This was rejected by the United States, which

## U.S. Armed Interventions in Panama, 1856–1903

| Year | Motive | Maximum No. of Troops | Duration in Days |
|------|--------|----------------------|------------------|
| 1856 | Watermelon War | 160 | 4 |
| 1860[a] | Local disturbance | 100 | 11 |
| 1861[b] | Political disturbance | — | — |
| 1865 | Political disturbance | — | 1 |
| 1868 | Riots | 14 | 1 |
| 1873 | Civil war | 200 | 15 |
| 1873 | Civil war | 190 | 13 |
| 1885 | Local disturbance | 12 | 1 |
| 1885 | Prestán/Aizpuru revolt | 1,200 | 57 |
| 1895 | Bocas del Toro | 70 | 1 |
| 1901[c] | Thousand Days War | 460 | 15 |
| 1902 | Bocas del Toro | 1 company | 7 |
| 1902 | Thousand Days War | 350 | 63 |
| 1903 | Independence | 42 | 3 |

Sources: Milton Offutt, *The Protection of Citizens Abroad by the Armed Forces of the United States* (Baltimore, 1928), 37–99, passim; Gerstle Mack, *The Land Divided* (New York, 1944), 163–68, 352–53, 440; Alfredo Figueroa Navarro, *Dominio y sociedad en el Panama colombiano, 1821–1903* (Panama City, 1978), 344–46; Alex Perez-Venero, *Before the Five Frontiers: Panama from 1821–1903* (New York, 1978), 115; E. Taylor Parks, *Colombia and the United States, 1765–1934* (Durham, N.C., 1935), 219; Colby M. Chester, "The Diplomacy of the Quarterdeck," *American Journal of International Law* 8 (1914): 443–76.
[a] By request and with British participation
[b] By request
[c] With French participation
— = data unavailable

claimed the prior applicability of the Bidlack-Mallarino Treaty. Since the British were already retreating from Central America and would relinquish their protectorate over Mosquitia in 1860, they were disappointed by the uncooperative attitude of the United States.[16]

Between 1848 and 1869, according to estimates by Kemble, 373,000 passengers traveled to California via Panama, and 224,000 made the return trip. Travelers stayed on the isthmus for between several days and several weeks and spent large amounts of money. This flow of foreigners represented a flood across the tiny province, where the 1843 census counted only 120,000 inhabitants. The amount of gold shipped back from California via Panama also reached dazzling proportions: $710 million in the same period.[17] This amount of traffic via a railroad that nearly defied engineers evoked great pride among the American people. The legend of American ingenuity and accomplishments in the tropics had begun. The impact on Panama, however, was not always as beneficial or welcome to the natives.

With the completion of the Panama Railroad, the United States clearly gained a transportation link of strategic military and economic importance. It tied together the East and West coasts until the transcontinental railroad could be completed, and even afterward it carried a great deal of traffic efficiently. Panama also became a regular port of call for the U.S. Navy, which projected the country's influence throughout the region. During the Civil War it moved troops and matériel between the oceans and brought gold with which the Union paid its bills.[18] Finally, the railroad gave U.S. citizens their first prolonged experience with operating an international facility in the tropics.

The U.S. government contributed decisively to the establishment of steamship lines to Panama with the Warship Act of 1847 and indirectly to the construction of the Panama Railroad. For example, public monies provided for the defense of the railroad under the authority of the Bidlack-Mallarino Treaty and paid for transport of the mails across the isthmus. Diplomatic representatives in Panama acted as agents of the railroad. The Panama route, then, was a publicly sponsored project critical to U.S. national and international expansion in the 1850s and 1860s and would remain so in the public mind long after its strategic value waned.

Panama also derived substantial benefits from the railroad and related steamship service. The value of land and labor in the transit zone soared, and unprecedented amounts of money circulated freely. The railroad united the central portion of the country with rapid rail and telegraph service. Talented and experienced entrepreneurs and workers came from all over the globe to start businesses and ply their trades, and many remained and established families. Not even in the heyday of the Spanish galleons had Panama been so prosperous.

People and cargo moving through seemed to satisfy the Panamanians' dream of becoming a crossroads of the world.

Many things detracted from the satisfaction Panamanians felt upon the completion of the railroad, however. The huge American community contained many enterprising and productive people, but they tended to be arrogant, greedy, demanding, insensitive, and contemptuous toward Panamanians. Many also displayed a virulent racism in their dealings with the local population, which was largely black and mestizo. They also became irritated at the political instability, the slow pace of life, and the cultural differences they neither understood nor appreciated. So the permanent American residents were rarely the considerate guests Panamanians expected.[19] This should not have been surprising—Americans dealt the same way with the nonwhite Indians and Mexicans whose lands they overran in the West.

Americans assumed that they were responsible for any and all progress in the land and that the Panamanians, left to their own devices, would slip into lethargic inaction. In their view, the Panamanians should have been grateful for the material development the railroad brought and should have aspired to become like Americans themselves. Americans' sense of superiority exempted them from behaving as guests in another land and justified their taking control of everything. Americans felt that Panamanians who did not appreciate what the Americans brought could simply melt back into the jungle.[20] In fact, Panamanians were industrious people, but their aspirations and work ethic differed from the Americans'.

The foreign community, and especially the transient Americans, also exhibited dissolute behavior rarely found at home. In the absence of the usual social restraints and sanctions, many indulged themselves in vices, mostly prostitution, drunkenness, and gambling. The gold fever and the dangers of travel seemed to exaggerate the moral abandon of many. A rich memoir and travel literature plus many surviving diaries attest to the wild and reckless behavior of the foreigners in Panama at this time. Well-to-do Panamanians deplored such things but could do little about them.[21]

A number of other developments caused anger and distress among the Panamanians in the 1850s. The importation of foreign labor was

one. In addition, many immigrants from Europe and the Andean republics arrived and established themselves in business. The local elite
accepted the most affluent of these outsiders and often allowed them
to marry into their families, but local folk who felt left out tended
to resent foreigners' upward mobility.[22] Yet another irritant was the
wholesale purchase of land in and around the transit zone by foreigners. The railroad and steamship companies gobbled up property
in downtown Panama City and on several outlying islands used as
anchorages. The resultant land squeeze drove up rents and often dis-
placed working-class families. Finally, the foreigners brought death
to the isthmus in the form of cholera and other diseases. To be sure,
Panama had its own macabre store of illnesses—malaria, dysentery,
smallpox, yellow fever, and tuberculosis—but the periodic cholera
epidemics, mysterious fevers, and venereal disease probably arrived
on visiting ships.

The violence displayed by resident or transiting Americans deeply
disturbed the Panamanians. Most travelers carried sidearms and
knives and often behaved aggressively toward the local population.
Moreover, during these same years William Walker and his filibuster
army attacked Baja California and later took over Nicaragua, events
that harkened back to pirate attacks in Panama during colonial times.
Rumors in 1856 that Walker's soldiers were on their way to Panama
proved unfounded but certainly contributed to feelings of distrust and
fear. Annexation by the United States was also a possibility. Ran Runnels's mass lynchings and vigilante executions violated Panamanians'
sense of justice, even though most deplored the banditry that inspired
them. While the Americans were certainly not responsible for all the
violence in Panama at the time, they seemed to provide more than
their share.

Finally, Panamanians experienced disappointment and even betrayal with the economic effects of the railroad. Except for the several
hundred persons it employed, most Panamanians received little direct
benefit from the railroad. In the words of one leader, it brought a "false
prosperity" because the goods and people flowed through and left few
material improvements in the land.[23] That was certainly the view of
the unemployed boatmen, muleteers, and carriers. Most of the lucra-

tive business the railroad generated was in the hands of foreigners. Therefore, the railroad, wrote one historian, did not contribute to the modernization of the country.[24] At the same time, the local economy rose and fell according to the railroad traffic and international business cycles in general. From the 1850s on, Panama experienced exaggerated boom and bust fluctuations.

The year 1856 proved especially wrenching to Panamanians, for the railroad now provided through service from Aspinwall/Colón to Panama City and inaugurated its steam lighter service in Panama Bay. Thousands of Panamanians found themselves out of work and unable to make a living in the depressed economy. A famous incident on 15 April 1856, called the Watermelon War, laid bare the tensions, fears, and anger Panamanians experienced due to the economic adjustments and foreign presence. Briefly, a drunken American bound for New York refused to pay for a slice of watermelon and was accosted by the vendor, a black man. The scuffle soon degenerated into a brawl between the Americans and Panamanians, most of them blacks. Within a few hours U.S.-owned businesses in the area lay in shambles and the Americans took refuge in the train station. Next the Panamanian police arrived on the scene and, after being shot at from the train station, attacked and eventually overran it. The mob destroyed the station, tore up track, cut telegraph wires, and terrorized the Americans, who were finally escorted aboard a steam tender and taken off shore. The casualties included fifteen Americans and two Panamanians dead and dozens of injured.

The effects of the Watermelon War lingered for years. In the hours and days following the riots, Panamanians became convinced that the Americans would retaliate by attacking and burning Panama City. No more fighting occurred, and the city settled back into its routine, but hostility lay just beneath the surface. The U.S. consul, meanwhile, blamed the police for the destruction of the railroad station and requested military occupation. Several months later, in response to political disturbances, 160 U.S. sailors landed in Panama City and stayed peacefully for three days before reembarking. This intervention, justified by the Bidlack-Mallarino Treaty, set several precedents and triggered a long and bitter dispute over reparations. The occupation meant that the United States was prepared to intervene in Panama to put down local disturbances, not just defend against foreign aggressors. Moreover, the United States used the Watermelon War to pressure Colombia in various ways on the pretext of indemnifying the victims. At first negotiators insisted on territorial concessions to the United States along the lines of what actually occurred a half-century later.[25] The matter dragged on for years until Colombia finally paid some $412,000. As Mack concludes, "Throughout the decade of negotiation and dispute the harsh arrogance of the United States government had embittered relations with New Granada."[26] The Watermelon War, then, was the first in a long series of clashes between Americans and Panamanians over their different worldviews and rights in the transit zone. The U.S. insistence on its jurisdiction led to diplomatic friction for years afterward, not to mention the personal animosities engendered. Finally, the sense of disappointment with the economic results of the railroad probably contributed to the rise of a secessionist movement in Panama from 1858 to 1863.[27]

An especially severe recession occurred after the U.S. transcontinental railroad began operating in 1869, one that demonstrated how Panama depended on the isthmian railroad for its livelihood. Panama lost about half its California passenger service because the railroad management did little to adapt to the new situation. Still, the steamship-rail route through Panama continued to offer competitive cargo rates, although it took longer than the direct train. In the 1870s a consortium of U.S. railroads, suffering from a contraction of freight at home, paid the Panama Railroad an annual fee to limit its shipments across the isthmus. This arrangement shifted business from Panama to U.S. carriers and frustrated Panama and Colombia. The slack business led Panamanians to resent the fact that only 10 percent of Bogotá's railroad annuity of $250,000 was transferred to the isthmus. Periodic rumors of secession circulated throughout the 1870s.[28]

The intense interaction between Panamanians and North Americans in the 1840s and 1850s established lasting patterns for U.S.-

Panamanian relations. They did not augur well for the future. All major decisions emanated from Washington, Bogotá, and New York. Several hundred thousand people made their way across the country, generating the kinds of interpersonal hostilities that poison relations between two countries. The local population felt put upon, exploited, and manipulated, while the foreign community prospered from the remarkable flow of gold and passengers yet displayed a condescending attitude toward the Panamanians. Ultimately, Panamanians and Americans did not develop much understanding of or tolerance for one another. Panama City may have become Americanized, as some historians remarked, but that was only a surface phenomenon. The Panamanian elite collaborated with the foreigners in order to get ahead, but the lower class remained sullen and resentful of the outside impositions. As one Panamanian wrote, "It continued to appear that Isthmian sacrifices were for the benefit of two foreign nations—Colombia and the United States."[29] Panama was forced into a partnership in an important enterprise—the Panama Railroad—but the rewards seemed to accrue mostly to the United States.

# 3    The French Period

On 18 August 1885 local authorities in Colón hanged a light-skinned mulatto named Pedro Prestán, ending one of Panama's bloodiest revolts of the nineteenth century. Months earlier, Prestán and another Liberal politician, Rafael Aizpuru, assumed control of Colón and Panama City to protest the election of Conservative Rafael Núñez in Bogotá. U.S. troops had landed and helped the Colombian forces to subdue the population, their largest foreign military undertaking between the Civil War and the Spanish-American War. The invasion reinforced U.S. determination to keep the peace in Panama, despite the ongoing French canal project. It also left bitter feelings among Panama's Liberals, who accused the United States of partisanship. Today Prestán is held up as a hero for resisting the gringos and sacrificing his life for Panama.

## American Initiatives

During the late 1860s and 1870s the U.S. government continued to pursue the possibility of building a canal in Central America, focusing first on Panama and then on Nicaragua. A French group headed by Ferdinand de Lesseps, meanwhile, gained the edge and won a concession to build a canal in Panama. For the next decade the French project captured world attention. Ultimately the effort failed, killed by poor engineering, disease, and mismanagement. The U.S. government, cool toward the French enterprise all along, moved increasingly in the 1890s to a decision to undertake a similar project with public monies. The number of surveys increased and a decision emerged to pursue an existing Nicaraguan concession or buy out the French rights in Panama. Out of the 1890s arose the American commitment to build a Central American canal.

The year 1869 was the *annus mirabilis* of the transportation revolution. Both the Suez Canal and the transcontinental railroad across the United States were completed. The U.S. government, recovering from the devastating Civil War of 1861 to 1865, began to give more attention to improving maritime transportation between the East and West coasts. The spirit of Manifest Destiny—muted during the war—revived in the administrations of Andrew Johnson and Ulysses S. Grant, and a Central American canal became an important component of that spirit.

President Grant tried very hard to conclude arrangements for building a canal in Central America. As a military man, he believed such a facility would enhance U.S. security, and he favored a canal under exclusive U.S. control and protection. He also thought it would contribute to human progress; as a young officer he had lost over one hundred soldiers and dependents to cholera in Panama, and he hoped a canal would help conquer the tropics. Further, he wished to go down in history as the creator of such a grand work. Finally, like most of his countrymen, he was suspicious of continued British influence in Costa Rica and Nicaragua.[1]

Talks regarding a canal treaty were already under way between Washington and Bogotá when Grant moved into the White House. The Colombians had regained canal rights from the Panama Railroad two years before and approached the State Department regarding a separate concession. With the impending completion of the Suez Canal, American interest in a Central American utility grew. In 1868 Secretary of State William Seward, described by one historian as an "arch expansionist," sent an agent to Bogotá with instructions to sign such a treaty. These negotiations serve as a benchmark for comparison to terms extended to the French in 1878 and to the United States in 1903.[2]

In general, the terms of the treaties signed by the United States and Colombia in 1869 and 1870 established that the canal would run through a twenty-mile-wide zone, with free port facilities at both termini. Alternating sections of land would be owned by Colombia and the builders (either the U.S. government or private U.S. interests).

This exclusive concession would run for one hundred years, and then the canal would revert to Colombian ownership. The waterway would be declared neutral in wartime, and other nations would be invited to recognize its neutrality. Still, canal protection was to be guaranteed by military forces of the United States acting jointly with Colombia. Any disputes between the parties would be resolved through arbitration. Colombia would receive 10 percent of the net profit from the canal operation until all the investment was amortized, after which its share would rise to 25 percent.[3]

Seward's instructions to his envoy regarding defense reversed the long-standing U.S. policy of favoring a neutral, internationally operated waterway. Instead, he requested exclusive operation and protection of the canal by the United States and Colombia. In the event of war, U.S. warships would have transit priority. The British government objected that these treaties violated the Clayton-Bulwer terms, which called for it to build the canal and guarantee its neutrality jointly with the United States. The State Department dismissed the protest on the same grounds it had before: Bidlack-Mallarino took precedence, and Clayton-Bulwer did not apply to Panama. The United States now sought "an American canal controlled by Americans."[4]

Meanwhile, the Colombian Senate rejected the first version on the grounds that it surrendered sovereignty to the United States and provided too little financial return to Colombia. Panamanian representatives in Bogotá, however, strenuously supported the treaty and insisted that it be rewritten, lest the province secede from the nation. Then the second treaty, embodying the defense alliance, was so heavily amended by Colombia that the United States tabled it.[5]

While attempts to reach a treaty with Colombia failed, U.S. officials undertook ambitious surveys of several Central American canal routes in the early 1870s and submitted them to the president's Interoceanic Canal Commission (ICC, 1872–76), the first of several such bodies.[6] The commission analyzed the surveys and in 1875 pronounced Nicaragua to be the better route, but it held that Panama was also viable. As for legal structure, the ICC recommended that the canal be neutral and operated by a consortium of maritime powers. This ran counter to Grant's preference for exclusive control, but his secretary of state, Hamilton Fish, convinced him to accept the proposed arrangement. Fish then sounded out the British, French, German, and Dutch governments and found no objection to proceeding on such a basis. So in 1875 the United States returned to its traditional position of international operation of the waterway.[7]

One of the main drawbacks to the Nicaraguan route was that Costa Rica and Nicaragua had not settled their dispute over the territories along the San Juan River, the Caribbean terminus of any canal there, so Fish opened talks with both countries regarding a canal concession. He envisioned a main treaty with Nicaragua and an ancillary one with Costa Rica agreeing to the use of the San Juan. The arrangement would provide for a neutral waterway with a surrounding zone under the control of an international board representing the maritime powers. The ocean within a five-mile radius of each outlet would also be neutral. Nicaragua would have virtually no say regarding the operation of the canal but was explicitly recognized as sovereign over the territory. Finally, the international consortium would come into being only after three nations signed agreements with the United States, and in wartime ships of countries that had not signed the neutrality treaty could be denied transit.

These talks proceeded slowly through late 1876 and early 1877 and then were broken off shortly before Grant's term ended. Neither Nicaragua nor Costa Rica liked the proposals, yet they had insufficient time to formulate counterdrafts. Nicaragua hoped to gain far more benefits from the treaty, including participation in canal operations, while Fish had reserved all operating responsibility for the international consortium.[8]

Even though the mid-1870s initiative failed, several important things had been accomplished. For the next quarter century the United States maintained an active canal option in Nicaragua, the preferred site in most American minds. In addition, a wealth of new data had been gathered by surveying expeditions. Finally, the State Department had temporarily embraced Grant's vision of a canal under exclusive U.S. control but then reverted to an internationalist stance.

Panamanians could hardly have taken satisfaction from the U.S. position in the 1870s, of course. They were under the economic and political control of the railroad, subject to military intervention by the United States, and about to be abandoned as a site for a canal. At that juncture, however, the French took up the Panama canal project and gave Panamanians new hope for their dream of becoming the crossroads of the western hemisphere.[9]

## The French Canal and U.S. Responses

The French group led by Ferdinand de Lesseps, who had directed construction of a sea-level canal at Suez in the 1860s, proceeded aggressively in the late 1870s to develop a plan and financing for a similar canal at Panama. It convened several conferences in Europe during those years to debate routes and engineering plans. American, German, British, and other delegates participated, but the French clearly held the initiative in these meetings. De Lesseps, a promoter and organizer rather than an engineer, was convinced that Panama possessed the best site and that he could build a sea-level canal there without locks, as he had done in Suez. The engineering meetings, in his view, merely served to raise public interest in the project and to provide scientific endorsement for his plans. U.S. delegates were quite critical of these efforts but could do little to dissuade de Lesseps.[10]

A French canal syndicate, formed in 1876, sent Lucien Wyse to Bogotá two years later to negotiate a contract with the Colombian government. The resultant concession granted the company the sole right to build and operate a canal in Panama for ninty-nine years, after which it would become the property of Colombia. It further stipulated that the facility must be completed in seventeen years. Colombia would receive an initial payment of 750,000 francs in 1882 and then, once the canal was open, a percentage of the gross revenues equal to at least $250,000 per year. The company received one-fifth of a kilometer of land on either side of the canal plus five hundred thousand hectares of additional land. The canal and terminal ports were to be neutral and open to the ships of all nations. The rights could be transferred to a private organization but not to a foreign government.

The Wyse Concession differed from the 1869–70 treaties with the United States in several ways. The duration and nonrenewable features remained, but the lands granted were not necessarily along the canal itself. And the facility would be neutral, rather than protected by the United States and Colombia.

Armed with this concession, de Lesseps convoked a Paris congress in 1879 to make final plans for the project. Strong-willed and persuasive, the organizer made sure that the delegates endorsed his plans for a sea-level canal along the route of the Panama Railroad. In the meantime, he gained assurances that he could buy a controlling interest in the Panama Railroad, essential for the project. The U.S. delegation voted against the plans and went home to report that the congress was rigged and the engineering unsound.

The U.S. government opposed the French canal undertaking yet could not find an incontrovertible reason for preventing it. The project did not technically violate the Monroe Doctrine, since it was undertaken by a private company with no military capability. The French government, however, was suspect because of its sponsorship of the disastrous Maximilian empire in Mexico. Moreover, de Lesseps had been portrayed as incompetent and overbearing by Americans who had dealt with him. Thus, for a variety of reasons, de Lesseps received a cool welcome when he spent a week in the United States lobbying for support.

President Rutherford Hayes, meanwhile, registered his objections in an 1880 message to Congress. He began: "The policy of this country is a canal under American control. The United States cannot consent to the surrender of this control to any European power." Although he spoke of control, he did not totally oppose ownership and commercial activities by private European interests, only their protection by military means. He indicated that such protection could not be shared and implied the right of the United States to review and approve a canal concession in the interest of its national defense. He even tried to gain Colombian acquiescence to this interpretation but failed.[11] Unvoiced, however, was his preference, shared by most Americans, that the canal be owned, operated, and defended exclusively by the United States.

Before leaving the United States, de Lesseps had arranged for several legal firms to represent him and his company, in court if necessary, in Congress, and before public opinion if the need arose. The company eventually expended some $2.4 million in legal fees in this way, most of it wasted, according to Mack.[12] Meanwhile, company agents left behind more cash when they managed to buy total control of the Panama Railroad. Several directors had cornered most of the stock after 1879 and eventually sold out to the company at over 100 percent profit in 1881. The total cash outlay was around $15 million. The railroad remained a New York corporation legally independent of the parent company, but the latter exercised its control through ownership of 99 percent of the stock. This was important, because it created another locus of support for the company in the American political scene.[13]

Hayes's secretary of state, James G. Blaine, later dubbed "Jingo Jim" by the press because of his strong aversion to European activities in the Americas, decided that the United States should abrogate the Clayton-Bulwer Treaty altogether. It infringed on the Monroe Doctrine and stood in the way of a canal under exclusive U.S. control. The opportunity to make this demand arose when Colombia approached several powers regarding a new joint treaty for the neutrality of the planned canal, one that would replace or supplement the Bidlack-Mallarino Treaty. Blaine served notice that the U.S. government regarded canal protection to be the sole responsibility of the United States and Colombia. When the British minister objected, Blaine suggested that Clayton-Bulwer was obsolete and should be amended. Besides, he concluded, it did not apply to Panama anyway.

The Clayton-Bulwer debate lasted for several months and ended inconclusively in 1883, after Blaine had been replaced.[14] Blaine had, however, introduced some important new principles regarding the U.S. posture toward transisthmian crossings and Latin America in general. First, Blaine reinterpreted the Monroe Doctrine as an injunction against meddling of any kind by European powers, including ownership of strategic resources (for example, a waterway or nitrates). Second, he emphasized the military reasons for the doctrine. Mary Wilhemine Williams points out, "For purposes of self-protection the United States claimed the right to control the isthmian transit, and offered by such control the absolute neutralization of the canal as respected European powers."[15] The Caribbean basin, then, was an American sphere of influence. Finally, the Monroe Doctrine according to Blaine sought to preserve the region for U.S. penetration, not merely to keep others out.

When the French syndicate, reorganized as the Compagnie Universelle du Canal Interocéanique in 1879, opened its capital subscription campaign, it received a disappointingly cool response from the middle-class investors to whom de Lesseps appealed. The first stock issue was an utter failure. The following year de Lesseps organized a second campaign, in which he attracted the participation of big banks and wealthy public figures with preferred stock while at the same time he sold millions of common shares to the French working class. This effort produced a bonanza, for the nation as a whole became convinced that the canal would be a vindication of the French genius and nationalism. The investors subscribed over twice the capital originally projected. The shady methods used to convince national leaders to support it, however, would lead to terrible corruption and scandals later.

The successful stock subscription of 1880 allowed de Lesseps to break ground in Panama in February 1881. Panamanians were ecstatic because it meant jobs, purchases, real estate appreciation, and the end of the 1870s recession. Even the more thoughtful believed that the French canal would make a reality of their dream to become a commercial emporium. A few dozen well-to-do Panamanians worked in the canal management, while thousands of the poor were hired as laborers. Migrant workers came from all over the Caribbean basin. Overnight, Panama hitched its wagon to the French star.

The division of labor during the French project resembled that of the railroad era. Panamanian families with money kept their assets in real estate and served as brokers for the French, while the latter snapped up the more transient but profitable businesses associated with supplying the canal and accommodating the foreign population.[16] As one historian notes, the economic and social distortions of the 1850s were amplified in the 1880s: labor scarcity, inflation, real-estate speculation, intermixing of elites, food shortages, and social unrest. A false sense of prosperity also prevailed.[17] On the other hand, the kind of interpersonal antagonism that plagued U.S.-Panamanian relations earlier seemed mostly absent, perhaps because of the greater cultural similarities that existed: Catholicism, Napoleonic law, artistic tradition, and romance language.

The demographic impact of the French project was far greater than that of the railroad. First, the construction went on for eight years before the company went bankrupt, and the work force swelled to many times what it had been in the 1850s. West Indian immigration probably reached a total of fifty thousand, and many thousands came from other parts of the world, including Africa. At one point the company payroll was nearly as large as the population of Panama City had been before construction began.[18]

Although the French obtained the canal concession from the Liberals in Bogotá, socially and philosophically they identified with the Conservatives in Panama. For one thing, the local Liberals tended to be racially mixed and commanded followings of blacks, mestizos, and mulattoes. Since the 1870s Liberal leaders on the Isthmus had been military caudillos whose manners were learned in the streets, barracks, and saloons. Intellectuals in the Liberal party tended to be lawyers, writers, and teachers, and they were staunchly anticlerical. Over the preceding decades mulatto Liberals had infiltrated local government and dominated the administration, where they controlled fiscal matters and the administration of justice. Finally, the Liberals tended to be more nationalistic and at times xenophobic.

The Conservatives, on the other hand, represented older families that prided themselves on Spanish lineage and white bloodlines. Most owned land in and around Panama City or in the interior, and most made their fortunes in commerce. They were faithful to the Church and valued Hispanic tradition. Finally, they welcomed foreigners to the point of appearing xenophilic.[19]

Politics in the mid-1880s disrupted the French canal work and Panama's relations with the United States. Since 1855 Panama had enjoyed special autonomy within the Colombian federation, a status that was reconfirmed during a six-month secessionist episode in 1861 and in the 1863 constitution. Politics during the 1860s and 1870s proved very tumultuous on the isthmus, however, due to local problems as well as civil wars in the rest of Colombia. President Rafael Núñez, in his second term, attempted to amend the constitution in order to strengthen his powers at the expense of the other branches and the states. This led to an outbreak of partisan warfare in 1884 that became generalized in 1885.[20]

In March 1885 two Liberal revolts broke out in Panama, those of General Rafael Aizpuru in Panama City and Pedro Prestán in Colón. Prestán, a federal deputy, ordered arms from the United States with which to strengthen his irregular force. When they arrived, however, the U.S. steamship agent refused to deliver them, and Prestán then took the agent, the U.S. consul, two naval officers, and several other Americans as prisoners. Prestán threatened to kill all Americans in Colón if the arms were not delivered. Since Colón was a company town owned by the railroad (and in turn by the French company), the largely foreign population and considerable property were in jeopardy. The U.S. naval commander impounded the arms and landed a hundred marines, at which point Prestán moved his soldiers and hostages outside of Colón. Colombian troops attacked Prestán, and after many hours of battle a fire broke out and swept through Colón, which was built almost entirely of wood.

The destruction of the city was blamed on Prestán, who fled to his native Cartagena but was eventually imprisoned, tried, and hanged.[21] Aizpuru, meanwhile, captured Panama City. At this point, the U.S. commander landed a thousand marines and sailors in Colón and moved most of them to the capital via the railroad. They soon arrested Aizpuru and elicited a pledge that he would not fight within the city limits or endanger the railroad—thereby respecting the Bidlack-

Mallarino Treaty. Eventually Aizpuru surrendered, complaining that the United States had sided with the Conservatives.[22]

The expeditionary force, the largest the United States had undertaken since the Mexican-American War, accomplished several important things. It asserted U.S. rights to guarantee transit on the isthmus even while the French were building their canal. It served notice to the Panamanians that they could not engage in civil disturbances that threatened foreign interests, American or European. Beyond such flag-showing impact, however, was a deeper change in U.S. activities in the region. The commanding officers, exceeding their authority from Washington, sought to establish a permanent naval patrol and possibly to gain rights to bases in Panama, and they used the press to generate public support. They sought information about Panama's offshore islands in case they decided "to occupy and hold them with an armed force." One writer calls the landing a "dress rehearsal" for the U.S. intervention in Panama's 1903 secession.[23]

Following the civil war U.S. citizens and the railroad presented claims for damages against Colombia amounting to $3.75 million, which the latter refused to pay. After five years the State Department abandoned attempts to collect.[24]

In 1886 President Núñez imposed a Conservative, centralist constitution on the nation that ran against Panama's interests. The semi-autonomous status ended; Catholicism became the official religion again; customshouses and high tariffs returned; and all governors were henceforth appointed. As a result, the U.S. consul wrote, three-quarters of the Panamanians would have preferred independence had they possessed the means to secure it.[25]

The political conflicts of 1885 cost the railroad several million dollars and disrupted canal work briefly, but other factors beyond Panamanians' control had already begun to undermine the canal project. Disease proved a formidable foe because workers from so many tropical regions brought illnesses that were then spread by mosquitoes. Only years later would medical experts test and implement mosquito control. As a result, perhaps twenty thousand canal workers died and thousands more suffered broken health.[26] Mismanagement also dogged the works, for de Lesseps and his directors spent lavish sums on public relations and goodwill and did little to economize. Eventually they ran out of money and were unable to raise new capital.

In the end, however, it seems that de Lesseps's insistence on a sea-level canal was the greatest obstacle to success. Looking back, it is clear that the project could never have been accomplished with the money, men, and machines at his disposal. Poor planning characterized every step of the way, and de Lesseps did not seem to know or care.[27] The first French project ended in 1888, when de Lesseps's company entered into receivership. It was a terrible blow to national pride, a financial disaster, and a political debacle that gave rise to the French term *un Panama* to signify great scandal.

The collapse of the company left some 13,000 West Indian laborers stranded in Panama in 1889, out of work and unable to return home. The British Colonial Office and the island governments eventually repatriated most, but the West Indians were left with a bitter memory of the experience. Many also elected to stay in Panama and were rehired by a successor French company after 1894. They and others became permanent immigrants in Panama, the beginning of a large West Indian community. They established homes, churches, mutual aid societies, and even rudimentary unions. Their presence in the 1890s, as afterward, provoked resentment on the part of some Panamanians, who would have preferred white European settlers.[28]

The U.S. government, meanwhile, had quietly applauded every French mishap and welcomed the collapse of the company. Throughout the 1880s the State Department kept alive its options in Nicaragua, where most Americans believed the canal should be built. After several false starts, initial construction actually took place on a Nicaraguan canal from 1889 to 1893. The effort was hamstrung, however, by disagreement over whether it should be undertaken by the government or a private company. In the end, the latter view prevailed, and Congress declined to vote a subsidy for the project.[29] The United States also continued to provide military protection for the Panama Railroad, still a U.S. corporation, and to preserve Colombia's sovereignty over the isthmus. The United States seemed to regard this responsibility with relish, far from a burden. Indeed, a consensus had emerged in Washington during the 1880s to the effect that the Clayton-Bulwer Treaty had to be scrapped to allow U.S. preeminence in the region.[30]

## The United States and the New French Canal Company

Throughout the 1890s knowledgeable observers assumed that once the French withdrew from the canal race, the United States would exercise its option to construct a canal in Nicaragua. The 1890s did not see definite progress in this direction, however, because of several factors. First, the receivers of the French company organized a new corporation and renewed its concession from Colombia, so Panama remained a potential site. Second, U.S. authorities remained divided over the issue of private versus public initiative. Third, the country was in the grip of a serious depression, so Congress could not reasonably appropriate large sums for a canal project. In the end it took the Spanish-American War of 1898 to push the United States into a decision to build the canal.[31]

The canal company bankruptcy of 1888 plunged France into a crisis and nearly paralyzed the country's finances. Gradually, however, a plan emerged to reorganize and finance the company, obtain an extension on the concession, and salvage as much of the investment as possible. In 1890 Lucien Wyse, who had negotiated the 1878 concession, returned to Bogotá to obtain an extension beyond the March 1893 expiration date. The job proved harder than he expected because the Colombians tried to extract more money than he could offer. Eventually, Panamanian delegates there, fearful that the project might be abandoned altogether, forced a compromise to award the company a ten-year extension. In return the company promised to take up the work by February 1894 and to pay Colombia ten million francs cash and five million francs in shares.[32]

In Paris, meanwhile, the receivers attempted to unravel the complex finances of the company amid trials, scandals, suicides, and political chaos. One agent, the liquidator, attempted to get a grip on the inventory and pull together major stockholders. The other, representing the small stockholders, fought to make sure the receivers salvaged something for his constituents. During the following three years the agents and others struggled to reconstitute the company, and eventually (with another brief contract extension) they chartered the New Panama Canal Company in 1894. The details of the arrangement, ably narrated by James Skinner, are not as important as the fact that the French investment in Panama was salvaged.[33]

The New Company's activities in Panama can be broken down into three periods: from 1894 to 1898 the workmen maintained the installations and continued excavation along the lines laid out during the late 1880s; from 1899 to 1902 the company altered its engineering plan but kept digging; and after 1902 (when the U.S. government became committed to buying the Panama route) the work force was reduced to provide only minimal maintenance. In addition, the railroad, one of the New Company's major assets, continued to carry passengers and cargo across the isthmus and also briefly operated steamships up the Pacific Coast to San Francisco. During the 1890s the New Company's receivers and directors walked a fine line between protecting their assets and pushing ahead with canal construction.[34]

Labor unrest and violence with racist overtones plagued the French works in the 1890s. Strikes broke out in 1894 and 1895 due to wage differentials between the canal and railroad gangs. Recruiters experienced difficulties attracting workers to Panama due to the mortality, lack of repatriation, and low wages compared with other projects in the region. A contingent of West Africans was so unhealthy the entire group was returned. These imported workers became a problem for Panama when they walked off their jobs and attempted to scrape out a living in Panama. Thus the labor force of the New Company remained small, at most several thousand men. These same labor and racial problems would recur in future years on the American canal works.[35]

In 1898 the New Company altered its design for the canal, moving to one that utilized several reservoirs along the Chagres for navigation and lock operation. New and more realistic calculations of costs and schedules were discouraging, so the company did not step up excavation on the new design. Instead, its representatives made their first offer to sell the works to the U.S. government, the only other potential builder at that point. The approach was ignored by the U.S. president, William McKinley, for a variety of reasons.[36] In view of this and the revised plans, the New Company negotiated with Colombia an extension of its final date of completion, from 1904 to 1910, at a cost of five million francs.[37] Events in the United States had meanwhile completely altered the international situation as far as the canal was concerned.

If 1869 had been a key date in the transportation revolution, 1898 was just as important politically, for it marked the emergence of the United States as a major contender for power. The president had reluctantly asked Congress to declare war on Spain that year in response to the martial spirit of Congress and the press. The trigger had been the sinking of the USS *Maine* in Havana harbor. The war proved one-sided and short, yet it launched the United States on a course of imperialism, Yankee-style, through the acquisition of Puerto Rico, the Philippines, and Guam as colonies and Cuba as a protectorate. Although the war vote was close, public and congressional support for the expansionist surge was overwhelming.[38] The consolidation of empire, in turn, made construction of a canal imperative.

American public opinion regarding a Central American canal had reached a consensus in the late 1890s, even though the means remained elusive. The sixty-eight-day voyage of the warship *Oregon* around Cape Horn in 1898 to join in the Battle of Santiago pushed canal support to a crescendo. Enough work and lobbying had been done to that point to virtually guarantee that an American canal would be built in Nicaragua.

A private company had carried out surveys and works in Nicaragua between 1889 and 1893, hoping to obtain government backing. In 1894 Congress appropriated money for the Ludlow Commission to study possible canal routes. The following year it recommended further studies in Nicaragua, the preferred site. In 1897 McKinley empaneled the first Walker Commission to carry out surveys, which were concluded in February 1899. Its findings further refined the costs and plans for a Nicaraguan canal. Partly for this reason, McKinley had not responded to the New Company's offer of two months before.[39]

In 1899 the battle of the routes began in earnest, pitting pro-Nicaragua forces against pro-Panama ones. By then, however, major public figures had decided that the government, and not a private company, should undertake construction of the canal. Yet the number of proposals, options, and vested interests was still large, and Congress had difficulty reaching a decision. The pro-Nicaragua group was led by Senator John Tyler Morgan, and the so-called Panama Lobby was headed by William Nelson Cromwell, of the New York law firm of Sullivan and Cromwell. Morgan, a southerner who chaired the Interoceanic Canals Committee in the Senate, had long advocated Nicaragua and seemed to have the votes as well as public opinion on his side. He pushed a bill through the Senate in 1899 authorizing the U.S. government to build, fortify, and operate a canal in Nicaragua. The bill was derailed in the House due to political rivalry. Morgan's opponents, meanwhile, in order to buy time, passed a bill calling for the Walker Commission to return to Central America in order to compare the Nicaragua and Panama routes.

Cromwell had been a minor shareholder in the Panama Railroad since 1881 and a director and legal counsel since 1893. In 1896 the New Company directors (who owned the railroad) retained Sullivan and Cromwell to conduct lobbying and public relations on behalf of their Panama operations but did not authorize much money for the effort. By 1898, however, the New Company unleashed Cromwell to do everything he could to sell the Panama canal to the U.S. government and to scuttle the Nicaraguan project.[40]

As Cromwell plotted and conspired, Philippe Bunau-Varilla, another prominent figure in the lobby, conducted an unofficial campaign to sway the American public in favor of the Panama route. Working separately and largely in secret, they eventually turned the tide in favor of Panama. Bunau-Varilla had worked on the canal under de Lesseps and then became managing engineer for Artigue, Sonderegger, and Company, a private firm that had contracted to excavate the canal in the late 1880s. The owners, who had made huge illegal profits from the canal, had been forced to invest in the New Company or go to jail. Bunau-Varilla represented this group plus his own substantial investment in the enterprise.[41]

The second Walker Commission issued three different reports comparing the Nicaraguan and Panamanian routes. In November 1900 it found against the latter because the French held the concession until 1910 and could not transfer it to a foreign government. Soon, however, the New Company and the Colombian minister gave the United States assurances it could indeed buy the concession from the New Company, for $109 million dollars. The price was too high, and a year later the Walker Commission recommended Nicaragua again, this time based upon the additional cost of acquiring the rights to the French canal. A canal at Nicaragua would require $189 million, while that at Panama would be $253 million ($144 million for the canal and $109 million for the French rights). The New Company immediately dropped its price to $40 million, at which point the commission issued a third opinion, this time in favor of Panama. Throughout its hearings, the members testified that they preferred Panama for several reasons—a shorter cut, better harbors, lower summit, an existing railroad, seismic stability, and the French excavations—but could not recommend paying the New Company's asking price.[42]

The Walker Commission's final verdict prompted Senator John C. Spooner to amend the Nicaraguan canal legislation then pending in the Senate so that the president would first approach Colombia to acquire rights for the transfer of the French company's assets and sign a suitable treaty with the United States for construction, fortification, and operation. If these attempts should fail, the president was then to proceed with a canal in Nicaragua. The amended legislation soon passed the Senate and was accepted by the House in June 1902.[43]

Several factors explained this abrupt reversal of congressional will. First, the new president, Theodore Roosevelt, believed that Panama was the superior site, and he was anxious to get work under way before he sought nomination for reelection in 1904. Second, Cromwell, an active Republican, had managed to swing GOP leader Marcus A.

Hanna around to favor Panama, partly with technical arguments and likely with campaign contributions. Hanna then helped bring his party over to that position. Third, a large number of congressmen became convinced during the long debates and testimony that the Panama site had advantages over that at Nicaragua. Obviously, this shift had profound implications for U.S. relations with Panama. It also affected U.S. ties with Britain.

As American commitment to build an isthmian canal increased in the late 1890s, both the State Department and the Foreign Office recognized that the Clayton-Bulwer Treaty would be an obstacle. In 1896, for example, Secretary of State Richard Olney stated that if the United States wished to build and fortify a canal in Central America, it should not use questionable interpretations of the treaty but should forthrightly negotiate a new agreement.[44] The British, for their part, were disposed to improve relations with the United States because of their relative isolation from the European powers and the need to respond to potential problems in their colonies. Therefore the two countries had agreed in 1898 to negotiate a replacement for the Clayton-Bulwer Treaty, and the following January Secretary of State John Hay produced a draft based upon the neutrality agreement for the Suez Canal. Throughout 1899 the matter drifted, as London tried to use it to pry concessions from Washington regarding a Canadian-Alaskan border dispute.

When a bill to construct and fortify a canal in Nicaragua made its way through Congress in early 1900, the Foreign Office decided to make unilateral concessions on Clayton-Bulwer in order to avoid embarrassments. Therefore, in February 1900 the British Ambassador, Sir Julian Pauncefote, signed a convention with Hay calling for the complete neutrality of any U.S. canal, along the lines governing Suez, which meant virtual demilitarization, even in time of war.

Some months later, however, the Senate sharply amended the treaty by taking out the Antifortification Clause and dropping the neutrality arrangements. Many Americans believed that the principal value of a canal would be military, so they insisted on the right to defend it. Roosevelt (while still governor of New York) proved a most effective critic, pointing out that an undefended canal would be a liability in wartime, whereas a fortified one would be a major strategic asset.[45] In view of the uproar, the British declined to accept the U.S. amendments.

After his succession to the presidency in September 1901, Roosevelt retained Hay as secretary of state and asked him to conduct new talks because of his great interest in building and fortifying a canal in Central America. This time Hay presented London with a draft that met most of the British objections yet also allowed the United States to fortify the canal. After some revisions by both sides, Hay and Pauncefote signed the treaty in late 1901. As signed and ratified, the new treaty spoke of neutrality but in fact permitted making the canal a U.S. military bastion.[46] While the measure smoothed U.S.-British relations, it would create new problems with Panama when the canal was actually built there.

## The War of a Thousand Days

Panamanians had been largely absent from the international negotiations conducted by the New Company, Colombia, the United States, and Great Britain. They chafed under the rule of the Conservative party, which controlled the central government in Bogotá. Isthmian businesses had to pay a myriad of taxes and fees and suffered under restrictive trade rules. The resurrection of the French project in 1894 did not spell prosperity for Panama, because of its managers' cautious, parsimonious policies. Still, Panamanians hoped that the French might be able to complete the canal or would cede the rights to the United States, the only viable successor at the time. They lived with the very real fear, however, that the United States might build the canal in Nicaragua, dashing their dreams of becoming a commercial emporium and condemning Panama to eternal poverty. Even the railroad would probably cease to be profitable if a canal opened in Nicaragua.

Many Panamanians doubted that government leaders in Bogotá could be trusted to negotiate such a crucial document as the canal concession. In their view, partisanship, corruption, personalism, and violence had characterized politics in Colombia for longer than they could remember. Thus the civil wars that broke out in 1899 and continued for three years—known as the War of a Thousand Days—sparked various emotions among the Panamanians. Some saw the war as yet another disruption of business and occasion for taxing Panama to sustain armies. Others viewed it as the ultimate breakdown of authority, the longest and bloodiest struggle in a long series of civil wars.[47] Still others saw it as an opportunity to restore some of the autonomy lost in 1886 or perhaps even to strike out for independence. As Perez-Venero notes, "Many Isthmians felt [Bogotá] treated Panama as only a colony instead of as an integral part of the Colombian nation."[48] The Thousand Days War, then, proved an important step in the events that led to Panama's independence and the construction of a canal there.

Briefly, Liberal chieftain Belisario Porras invaded Chiriqui province in March 1900 and captured the city of David. Within three months he and his military commander had moved their armies to the outskirts of Panama City and attacked the capital. They failed due to poor cooperation between Porras and his officers, and the former went into exile again. In mid-1901 Porras managed to put together another Liberal army, this time in Costa Rica, and he captured a major city in the interior. There he linked up with a charismatic warrior, Victoriano Lorenzo, and his cholos (mixed-blooded irregulars), and with the army of Gen. Domingo Díaz. In September they took Chorrera, some fifteen miles west of the capital. The Colombian government, meanwhile, warned foreign consuls that it would not be able to maintain law and order in Panama due to the fighting and requested U.S. military intervention to restore peace. The Panama Railroad managers also complained of Liberal army misuse of the line to transport supplies and troops. In November 1901 the United States landed marines in Colón and took the city back from the Liberals.

In December 1901 another Liberal general, Benjamín Herrera, arrived in Panama, and within two months he and the local rebels were poised to capture Panama City and Colón. The U.S. forces in the theater again deployed to prevent a Liberal victory. The rebels, who could count on the loyalty of the majority of the Panamanians, held the military advantage and had captured much of the interior of the province in 1902. By then Herrera had some nine thousand men and modern weapons and could easily have taken the capital. Again, the U.S. authorities in Panama warned him not to attack the terminal cities or disrupt railroad service. In the end, Herrera and the others were forced to give up the struggle in October 1902 because outside the transit zone they had no military targets of strategic value. In November Herrera signed a peace treaty on board the U.S. battleship *Wisconsin*.[49]

While most Liberal commanders returned to their peacetime occupations, the guerrilla chieftain Lorenzo was put to death by a firing squad. Horrified Liberals blamed the Conservatives (and by extension the Americans) for violating the treaty, whereas the government claimed that Lorenzo was a common criminal and hence not under treaty protection. Lorenzo was elevated to the status of martyred hero by later generations.[50]

The Thousand Days War affected U.S.-Panamanian relations in important ways. First, it weakened the Colombian government and forced it to renew the French company's concession. This set the stage for a U.S.-French accord. Second, it disrupted talks with the United States regarding the Panama route and exposed Colombia's inability to maintain the peace there. Third, it gave rise to almost continuous intervention by the United States to prevent a rebel victory or secession. Thus the United States became allied with the Panamanian Conservatives during these turbulent years. Finally, by emphasizing the risks of civil war it increased pressure for a zone that could isolate the canal from threats of violence.

There is no doubt that the U.S. military interventions occasioned by the Thousand Days War prevented a Liberal victory in Panama and perhaps in the country as a whole. On the other hand, if the Liberals had taken Panama and the Conservatives held the rest of the country, it might have led to Panama's secession a year earlier and at the hands of the Liberals, instead of in 1903 led by the Conservatives.[51] So, as Alex Perez-Venero observes, the war left "a financial and spiritual scar" on Panama and moved it a long step closer to independence.[52]

By 1902 the situation in Panama had changed dramatically from what it had been in the late 1860s, yet it was by no means settled. The railroad had lost its near-monopoly on trade between the East and West coasts of the United States and had been purchased by the French company that attempted to build a canal in the 1880s. Indeed, the strong U.S. presence in Panama diminished, replaced by the French, and what remained was largely to enforce the terms of the Bidlack-Mallarino Treaty. Panama had lost its autonomy in the 1880s, meanwhile, when the Conservatives seized the government in Bogotá and centralized power. Colombian politics, as played out in Panama, exacerbated feelings of mistreatment and anger. The frequent civil wars, disruption of trade, taxation, and impositions of officials appointed by Bogotá led to desires for independence. It was precisely this unsettled state of affairs in Panama, as well as the failure of Bogotá to reach a canal agreement with the United States, that led to the fateful events of 1903.

# 4    Canal Diplomacy, 1902–1919

On the evening of 18 November 1903, in Washington D.C., two figures bent over a desk to examine a document. At about 7 P.M. John Hay, U.S. secretary of state, had invited Philippe Bunau-Varilla, a Frenchman representing the newly independent Republic of Panama, to sign a treaty they had both drafted. They read it, discussed some clauses, penned a few changes, and then signed it. Thus began the formal U.S.-Panamanian alliance. For the next three-quarters of a century that document would evoke criticism, anger, and sometimes violence from Panamanians; Americans stood by its terms, for the most part, insisting that it was a binding contract. Under its aegis the United States built and operated one of the great transportation facilities in the world: the Panama Canal.

## The Second Independence of Panama

From the 1890s until the end of World War I, the United States rose in status from a regional to a world power. This rise took place in stages: growing influence throughout the hemisphere by means of the Pan-American movement; expansion of U.S. commercial rights in the Far East through the Open-Door notes; assertion of protectorate rights in the Caribbean basin during and after the Spanish-American War; and attainment of major-power status during the First World War. U.S. diplomacy in this era is sometimes labeled "imperialist" because of the acquisition of overseas territories (Hawaii, the Philippines, Puerto Rico, Guam, and the Virgin Islands) and the exercise of military dominion beyond its borders. The independence of Panama and the construction of the Panama Canal were an integral part of the U.S. rise to power.[1]

By mid-1902 the Roosevelt administration had the legislation it needed to proceed with negotiations for building a canal in Panama. The Spooner Act, however, had set certain conditions on the president: he could only pay $40 million to the New Company; the canal was to have a six-mile-wide zone in which to operate; the concession would be in perpetuity; and an agreement had to be reached within a reasonable time. Congress thus limited the scope of negotiations in important ways.

The Colombian government expected to reap huge rewards from a canal built in its Panamanian province, but formidable obstacles worked against it. For one thing, rebellious Liberals controlled most of the Panamanian province throughout 1902, and the central government was unable to defeat them. For another, powerful interests in Paris, New York, and Washington conspired to deprive Colombia of her just rewards or even her isthmian province. And finally, public opinion in Bogotá was running against an agreement with the United States, and politicians had become factious about canal matters in general.

Conservative José Manuel Marroquín, who had seized power by a coup in 1900, had his hands full managing negotiations in Washington, civil war in Panama, and politics at home. Marroquín was in no hurry to deal. He and most Colombians intended to force the New Company to pay for the right to transfer its concession to the United States. Another option was to nullify the 1904–10 extension of the New Company's concession, so that the works and equipment would become national property in only two years. Then a more lucrative deal could be struck with the United States. And of course Marroquín had to stiffen his agents in Washington in order to secure the best terms possible in the treaty.

Roosevelt, on the other hand, regarded the canal as his entrée into the history books and his greatest reelection plank for 1904, and he pushed to reach a canal agreement with Colombia quickly. Negotiations began in early 1902, even before Congress had passed the canal legislation. The Colombian government did not provide consistent or reasonable guidance for its representatives in Washington, and behind the scenes Bunau-Varilla and Cromwell were doing everything they could to protect the New Company's interests. Several treaty drafts were prepared and then abandoned due to disagreements between Washington and Bogotá.

Bunau-Varilla also began machinations in Panama, where he urged prominent figures to pressure Bogotá to conclude a treaty favorable to the New Company. He struck a note he knew would jar local sentiments: the politicians in Bogotá might ruin this great opportunity to secure a canal in Panama, in which case the United States would build one in Nicaragua. In that case, he intimated, Panama would be better off independent, so that it could make its own deal with the colossus. Oddly enough, Marroquín appointed as governor in Panama José Domingo de Obaldía, known to sympathize with independence, probably to frighten hard-liners in Bogotá into a more conciliatory mood.

The negotiations dragged on through the last half of 1902, until finally a treaty was signed in January 1903 between Secretary of State John Hay and the secretary of the Colombian legation, Tomás Herrán. The Hay-Herrán Treaty provided for transfer of the French works and equipment, a six-mile-wide canal zone (excluding the terminal cities of Panama City and Colón), a hundred-year renewable lease, shared jurisdiction and civil administration, a $10 million lump-sum payment, and an annuity of $250,000 upon completion of the canal. The U.S. Senate ratified the agreement in March.

The Colombian Senate, however, did not take up the Hay-Herrán Treaty until July, and then it deliberated for over a month. Finally, the Colombians rejected it. A number of objections produced a unanimous negative vote. The financial aspects seemed inadequate, in view of the $40 million to be paid to the French company and the $250,000 annuity previously derived from the railroad. E. Taylor Parks estimated that the Colombians stood to lose $50 million in income under the terms of Hay-Herrán.[2] Guarantees of Colombia's sovereignty in the Canal Zone, despite treaty references, seemed inadequate. And in a general way neither Panama nor Colombia seemed likely to benefit sufficiently.

The delay weighed heavily in Washington, where rumors of a con-
spiracy to promote the independence of Panama circulated openly.
The White House would not countenance amendments, postpone-
ment, or reduction in payment to the French company. Nor would
Roosevelt agree to take up the technically inferior Nicaraguan route
again. The canal at Panama had become an *idée fixe* in his mind. Unfortunately for him, the 1846 Bidlack-Mallarino treaty still pledged the
United States to uphold Colombia's sovereignty over Panama. Legally,
he could neither foment independence nor even sanction such a move.
It would have to be done covertly.

Ultimately, the Panamanian elite figured prominently in resolving
the 1903 impasse in canal negotiations. They had watched events
largely from the sidelines, in hope of seeing their dream of an
interoceanic waterway become a reality. Most supported the French
company's position, that the U.S. government take over the project,
though the Liberals warned against becoming a U.S. colony. Panamanians expected most of the indemnity money to disappear in Bogotá,
but they planned to reap great profits by selling supplies to the
Americans and from international trading.[3]

The Colombian Senate's protracted debate over the Hay-Herrán
Treaty sorely tested Panamanians' loyalty. Liberals saw their
autonomy being sacrificed to the United States. Conservatives feared
that rejection of the treaty would lead to a U.S. canal in Nicaragua.
Thus, in mid-1903 a number of prominent Conservatives, mostly men
of good standing connected to the Panama Railroad, began plotting
their separation from Colombia. In this they were secretly abetted
by Cromwell, who effectively managed the railroad's interests from
his New York offices. The conspirators chose elder statesman Manuel
Amador Guerrero to sound out U.S. authorities and to assume leadership of the revolt should it go forward. Amador sailed for New York
in August and met repeatedly with Bunau-Varilla. Cromwell, meanwhile, sailed for Paris to avoid revealing his role and exposing the
New Company and the railroad to expropriation by Colombia.

The Frenchman shuttled back and forth between the interested parties, principally Hay and Amador, and in two weeks he managed to set up the revolution. His meetings with Roosevelt and Hay convinced him that the U.S. government would recognize and protect an independent Panama. He persuaded Amador of this and supplied him with a declaration of independence, military defense plans, a communications code, and a flag. Bunau-Varilla even set the date, 3 November, to coincide with by-elections in the United States. The money Amador would need—$100,000—would be sent later, on the condition that Amador appoint Bunau-Varilla minister plenipotentiary of the new republic to the United States.

Amador returned to the isthmus and set in motion the events that would lead to Panama's independence and an American canal. The Panamanian conspirators, though disturbed by a lack of overt support from the U.S. government, went ahead with plans for a 3 November revolt on the assurances of Amador, his forceful wife, and a few others. Local bankers advanced cash (against Bunau-Varilla's promised funds) to suborn the local garrison. The railroad managers helped plan the revolt and played important roles in its outcome. As it turned out, the revolt came off as expected, with virtually no bloodshed.

The U.S. government supplied the muscle for the Panamanian conspiracy, despite efforts to cover up this role. Bunau-Varilla was encouraged to believe that an independent Panama would be protected and recognized immediately by the United States, as indeed occurred on 6 November. The USS *Nashville* arrived in Colón the day before the revolt and received orders to prevent hostilities on the part of any forces, including Colombian troops. In the days following the revolt, several other warships arrived to protect the fledgling nation. Panama would not have survived without this naval guarantee.

The Colombian government was devastated by the secession of Panama and immediately sought to strike a deal with the United States. They also sent an armed force overland to try to dislodge the new regime, but it did not arrive. The Colombian overtures, though never accepted by the United States, were important because they allowed Bunau-Varilla to warn the Panamanians that the United States might return to the status quo ante and negotiate a treaty with Colombia. Such a move would have spelled disaster for the independence leaders.

## The 1903 Treaty

Hearing of Bunau-Varilla's plans to sign a treaty, Panama's new leaders revoked the Frenchman's credentials but soon restored them under threat of withdrawal of U.S. protection. In Washington Hay and Bunau-Varilla moved quickly to consummate a treaty before the Panamanians could organize themselves. They worked from a version of the Hay-Herrán Treaty that Senator Morgan had amended to provide such exaggerated benefits to the United States that it would be bound to be rejected by Colombia.[4] Hay and his aides reworked this draft, confident that the Panamanians could not object as the Colombians would have. He also knew that Bunau-Varilla had a great personal stake in its execution, which would vindicate his efforts over the years. In essence Hay wrote a treaty that incorporated everything the United States could possibly want.

To begin with, the new draft expanded the zone from six to ten miles in width, added several offshore islands to it, and authorized the United States to take any other land it deemed necessary for the operation and defense of the canal. The United States likewise became the sole protector of the canal and its auxiliary installations, rather than a partner as before. The concession would last "in perpetuity," whereas the Hay-Herrán treaty stipulated a hundred-year renewable lease.[5] The United States would guarantee the independence of Panama.

Nowhere did the draft recognize Panama's sovereignty in the zone, the administration of which fell solely to the United States. In effect, the zone, more than five hundred square miles, would become an exclusive U.S. territory through the heart of Panama.

Bunau-Varilla received the Hay draft in mid-November and added some elements of his own. He retained the financial terms of the Hay-

Herrán treaty, that is, a $10 million indemnity and $250,000 annuity. He stipulated that Panama City and Colón remain outside the zone, though the United States would be empowered to keep the peace and provide sanitation there. Far and away the most controversial (and harmful from Panama's point of view) change was Bunau-Varilla's clause that finally read, "Panama grants to the United States all the rights, power and authority . . . which the United States would possess and exercise if it were the sovereign of the territory . . . to the entire exclusion of the exercise by the Republic of Panama of any such sovereign rights, power, or authority." In other words, Panama retained residual sovereignty but the United States gained effective ownership.

The counterdraft by Bunau-Varilla and that of Hay were discussed, and the former was adopted with only minor changes on 18 November. In effect, they had each tried to outbid the other in giving more advantages to the United States. Unfortunately for future relations, no one defended Panama's interests in these negotiations, so the treaty proved highly injurious to the young country. For this reason, Panamanians soon came to regret the deal made in their behalf.

The principals hurried through the formalities, because a week earlier a Panamanian delegation had sailed for the United States with credentials to negotiate and sign a treaty. They did not know that in the meantime the Frenchman had had their powers nullified. The delegation was within hours of arriving in Washington when Hay and Bunau-Varilla signed the fateful document on the evening of 18 November. From the Panamanians' point of view, Bunau-Varilla gave away their country's most precious resource—the best isthmian site for a canal—for a pittance. In fact, he had callously traded it for their independence.

Ratification of the treaty proceeded quickly. The Panamanian delegation had first refused to endorse the document but then agreed to send it to Panama. Bunau-Varilla cabled authorities there to say that if the treaty was not ratified immediately the United States would withdraw its protection, allow the Colombians to take the isthmus, and deal again with Bogotá. The threat worked, for the Panamanians approved the treaty on 2 December. The U.S. Senate also sanctioned the document, in late February 1904.

The method of reaching the treaty, however, and the overwhelming advantages obtained by the United States under it, would sour relations between the two countries and create bad feeling for generations. The canal would become a foreign enclave in the heartland of the country, from which the colossus of the north would dictate policy to the weak new republic.

In one early move, however, the U.S. government corrected the aspect of the treaty most damaging to Panama's immediate interests, economic isolation. In 1897 Congress had passed the Dingley Tariff, which erected protectionist barriers throughout the country. The law was applied to the Canal Zone in 1904, effectively sealing off Panama from the commercial opportunities created by the zone. Panama thus lost access to direct foreign trade in her principal cities and revenues from customs duties. The Interoceanic Canal Commission (ICC) also authorized zone residents to operate businesses that could reexport to Panama and elsewhere. Panamanian politicians and merchants protested so loudly that Roosevelt declared it was not his intention to create a commercial entrepôt in the Canal Zone. Secretary of War William H. Taft went to the isthmus and there signed the Taft Agreement, which dropped the tariff wall around the zone and allowed Panamanians access to ships anchored in canal harbors. Panama, for its part, guaranteed free movement of people and goods to and from the zone and adopted the gold standard, which in practice meant U.S. currency.[6]

Colombia of course never forgave the United States for abetting Panama's independence and taking over a major national resource. The State Department finally worked out a face-saving treaty and an indemnity payment of $25 million in 1921 to put the episode behind the two countries.[7]

## The Construction Era and World War I

In May 1904 Panama formally transferred to U.S. jurisdiction the zone embracing the future canal. At the same time the U.S. Treasury disbursed $10 million to Panama and $40 million to the New Panama Canal Company, through the fiscal agent for both, J. P. Morgan & Company of New York. The way was thus clear to begin the massive work of building the canal.

Over the next ten years the U.S. government, through the ICC, supervised the largest construction project of its kind in history, one of the great marvels of the world.[8] After weighing several alternative designs, the ICC adopted a locks and reservoir approach that had first been proposed decades before. The challenge was enormous: the terrain rose steadily from the Atlantic Coast to the continental divide, about 40 miles to the south, and then dropped sharply to the Pacific. The divide required moving vast amounts of rock and dirt to bring the canal level down to a reasonable height. On the other hand, neither of the two rivers that flowed north and south were navigable for more than a few miles, and seasonal flooding would not allow channelizing them.

The problem was solved by damming the Chagres River several miles inland in order to create a great lake (named Gatun) eighty-five feet above sea level. Ships would enter from the Atlantic by a conventional canal, then be raised to the lake by means of three sets of locks. Once on the lake the route followed the Chagres Valley to the point that it veered east. From there until the descent to the Pacific, ships would transit a totally man-made cut, eventually named Gaillard after a chief engineer. Finally, the ships dropped eighty-five feet to the Pacific in three more sets of locks. Total excavation for the canal amounted to more than a quarter-billion cubic yards.[9] The landscape of central Panama would never be the same again.

The works themselves staggered the imagination. The entire canal formed a system that required very little man-made power. Gatun Lake, supplied by the upper Chagres, flooded Gaillard Cut and filled the locks. Water released from the higher locks flowed by gravity into the lower locks to lift ships. The huge lock gates were so well-balanced that small electric motors could swing them at slack water. Because ocean-going vessels were so unmaneuverable in close quarters, they were towed through the locks by powerful electric locomotives, called mules. In the Cut and Gatun Lake, however, ships could proceed under their own power. The double locks permitted two-way traffic, and the average transit took eight to ten hours. The canal was a truly extraordinary work of engineering for the day.

Two parallel governments were set up in 1904, one for Panama and the other for the Canal Zone, as the construction area became known. The two governments maintained headquarters within blocks of each other in the old section of Panama City, until a canal administration building in Balboa was finished some time later. No one doubted that the canal officials wielded far more power than the Panamanian government. The relationship between them was that of protector and ward.[10]

The ICC proved an unwieldy arrangement, which Roosevelt and William Taft tried to dismantle but which Congress kept intact via the budget. In his last year as president, Roosevelt concentrated power in the hands of a chairman–chief engineer, Col. George W. Goethals, of the Army Corps of Engineers. Goethals managed the works as a virtual dictator until 1916. Still, the ICC continued to exist throughout the construction period. Goethals abhorred it, writing, "The whole definition of a board is applicable to a Commission, namely, it is long, narrow and wooden."[11] But if the U.S. administration was awkward, the new Panamanian government seemed chaotic.

In December 1903 the Panamanian Junta held elections for a constitutional convention to create a permanent government. During January the assembly established a centralized regime with a unicameral legislature and presidentially appointed provincial governors. The most controversial item in the new constitution, Article 136, gave the United States the right to use troops to keep the peace in Panama, much as did the Cuban constitution of 1901. Conservative leaders and the U.S. minister to Panama, William Buchanan, favored the measure, while Liberals disapproved.[12]

The assembly elected Manuel Amador as president and transformed itself into a legislature in order to pass emergency measures and to codify the country's laws. In June it disbanded, leaving Amador free to govern alone until a new legislature could be convened. The president did not want for advice, however. Minister Buchanan took it upon himself to call him over to the legation whenever he had matters to discuss.[13]

Early U.S. policies and actions in Panama varied greatly with the personnel in Washington and Panama City. In a general way, however, U.S. agents tried to concentrate their energies on the priority task of building a canal. They visualized the zone as an American compound quite separate from Panama, in which they could get on with the grand enterprise. They did have two important concerns with regard to Panama, though: sanitation and political stability. Tropical disease, as the United States had learned in Havana, could decimate an army more readily than hostile troops. And political turmoil in the republic could disrupt canal construction and hamper labor recruitment.

The sanitation of Panama, under the supervision of Col. William C. Gorgas, is a fascinating chapter in inter-American relations, one repeated in many other tropical countries.[14] In the late 1890s and early 1900s public health physicians had proven that malaria, yellow fever, and other diseases were transmitted by certain mosquito species, and they had devised means of locating and killing vector insects in their larval stage. Within a few years tropical cities that had been racked by pestilence were rendered healthful by these methods. Colonel Gorgas oversaw their application in Panama.

Both humanitarian and practical motives drove the sanitation programs. U.S. Army and public health doctors often cooperated in disease-control programs in areas where the army was active. It took little manpower and created goodwill. In addition, sanitation raised morale of troops posted in the tropics and kept them more fit for duty. In the case of Panama, authorities from Roosevelt on down regarded sanitation as essential for canal construction. Many blamed disease for the French failure two decades earlier.

The public health program consisted of three parts: water and sewage systems for the terminal cities, hospital construction, and mosquito control. The first would prevent the spread of bacterial illnesses and provide a healthier environment for tens of thousands of canal laborers who lived outside the zone. The canal hospitals, meanwhile, provided the first modern medical care available on the isthmus. (President Porras would inaugurate the first Panamanian hospitals in the 1910s.) The mosquito campaign benefited Panamanians, of course, but it also protected Americans and other foreigners living in the zone from insect-borne diseases. The effects of these campaigns were remarkable: within a few years Panama became a healthy place to live.

Political stability was harder to achieve for both Panamanian and American authorities, which is why less is written about it. Throughout the construction years, U.S. spokesmen made it clear that revolutions and violence would not be tolerated. Taft himself wrote in 1906, "It has been necessary . . . for the U.S. government to . . . advise all political parties in the Republic of Panama that in order to avoid obstruction to the building of the canal, the United States will not permit revolutions in that republic."[15] Since the zone bordered large concentrations of population, the two intimately affected one another.

Peacekeeping was the first priority. Theoretically, Panamanian police kept order in Panama City and Colón, while Canal Zone police did the same in their jurisdiction. In fact, American authorities never trusted their Panamanian counterparts and kept them on a short leash. The first step was the so-called demilitarization, whereby President Amador (with U.S. backing) disbanded his small army in 1904 and created the National Police in its stead. Then in 1916 the U.S. Navy confiscated rifles used by the National Police so that they would not pose a threat to the peace. From 1917 until the early 1930s the U.S. government supplied the police with an instructor, who attempted (ineffectually) to supervise law enforcement in the republic.[16]

Zone police and U.S. military authorities guarded the canal compound exclusively and could be reinforced by troops brought down from the United States. The colorful George Shanton, a figurative heir to Ran Runnels, organized the police in the early years with his flamboyant style and intimidating violence.[17] In 1912 the zone police consisted of 117 white Americans and 116 black West Indians, who kept the peace within their respective racial groups. In 1917 the U.S. government put the Canal Zone on a war footing under the commanding general of the army garrison there, and created the Panama Canal Department, an autonomous unit for canal protection. Henceforth the whole isthmus would be protected by this force and the dozen military bases created later.[18]

In the early years it was not obvious which laws would be enforced in the Canal Zone. The Hay-Herrán Treaty had provided for Colombian, U.S., and mixed courts, but that had been dropped in the Hay–Bunau-Varilla treaty. Gradually zone jurists codified a unique body of laws, that were administered by a small judicial system. The Canal Zone code eventually promulgated in 1934 drew on Colombian and North American precedents, but it was applied according to common-law methods and jury trials. The creation of a separate judiciary in the zone further alienated it from Panama.[19]

U.S. policy toward Panamanian politics evolved, going from indifference to protective paternalism during the construction era to outright domination in the war years. American authorities doubtless would have preferred not to deal with Panama at all beyond matters of sanitation and public order, but that was not feasible given the proximity of the terminal cities to the zone and the unequal relationship between the two countries. Several goals were evident in U.S. policymakers' actions. They wished Panama's elites to conduct themselves in a decorous, constitutional, and respectable manner, in part because the rest of the world regarded Panama as a U.S. ward. They also wanted Panama's leaders to be cooperative when it came to matters affecting canal construction, maintenance, operation, and defense. For their part, Panamanians expected to be treated with respect and dignity, as citizens of a sovereign nation, and to earn financial rewards from the canal, which they regarded as their greatest natural resource. Both sides were to be disappointed.[20]

The earliest form of political intervention in Panama was election

supervision. Conservatives had controlled the government since independence, with the support of the United States, yet the Liberals had a
large popular base. The latter urged U.S. authorities to guarantee hon-
est voting or at least to specify what steps they would take to prevent
election violence. Secretary of War Taft, who held line responsibility
for the canal project, and Secretary of State Elihu Root, resisted these
entreaties, and when they did station gunboats at Panama during the
June 1906 congressional and municipal elections, it was to prevent
a Liberal victory. The Conservatives won the contest, but violence
led to several deaths and to justifiable charges of fraud and intervention. Liberals began to speak openly of a revolt against the Amador
regime.[21]

In 1908 Taft, himself candidate for the U.S. presidency, decided to
use army officers as marshals to supervise the presidential election in
Panama. The United States also played this role in the 1912 and 1918
elections. After that, however, the United States declined requests to
monitor elections until the late 1980s.

Election supervision led inevitably to deeper involvement. In 1908
Taft actually dictated the succession in Panama. The Liberal candidate won when his opponent withdrew because of the U.S. role. The
messiest case occurred in 1910, when the U.S. chargé, Richard Marsh,
and the chairman of the ICC, Colonel Goethals, pressured the incumbent (the popular and able Carlos A. Mendoza) to bow out of
the presidency because he was a mulatto. Marsh then tried to dictate
the succession to the legislature, or in his own words to "ram [his
candidate] down their throats." He acted so openly and clumsily that
Goethals and the State Department repudiated his actions, and he
was called home in disgrace.[22]

The most drastic form of U.S. intervention was military occupation
of Panamanian territory. This occurred in June 1918 in order to force
the government to hold elections they had tried to postpone and then
to supervise the balloting. Soon after the elections, U.S. Army forces
took over Chiriqui province along the Costa Rican border in order to
protect an American landowner accused of murdering the governor.
That occupation lasted until August 1920 and left a residue of bitter-

ness among all Panamanians. From then until 1989, U.S. troops would only intervene when invited.[23]

The zone commander who ordered the occupation, Gen. Richard Blatchford, for a time waged a moralistic and (for the Panamanians) humiliating campaign to clean up vice in the terminal cities. Claiming that these were worse than Sodom and Gomorrah, he banned soldiers from red light districts and tried to deport prostitutes from Panama. He also outlawed liquor and tried to stiffen police surveillance in the zone.[24]

Despite the Taft Agreement, the Canal Zone developed a fairly self-sufficient economy. For one thing, the railroad continued to function as a private corporation, importing merchandise and operating commissaries and shops. Most major merchandise wholesaling in the zone, construction (even in Panama), and industrial development was conducted by Americans or other foreign nationals. Little control was exercised, so that anyone could acquire goods and services in the zone. Repeated protests by merchant associations and the foreign ministry failed to halt these practices.[25] As a result, the Panamanian bourgeoisie had only a few means of cashing in on the construction boom: they built rooming houses, saloons, brothels, restaurants, and shops along the zone border to cater to soldiers and to the foreign labor force imported to build the canal. Some Panamanians amassed wealth in these activities, but not nearly as much as they had hoped.

The foreign labor presence had a profound impact on Panama, about which the two countries disagreed almost constantly. The 1903 treaty authorized the United States to import construction workers freely. A majority of the immigrants—whether contracted directly by the canal or arriving on their own—lived in the terminal cities. Most were West Indian blacks from Barbados and Jamaica, but men and women from scores of other nationalities and ethnic groups were drawn to Panama. Eventually the Panamanian elite became displeased with the large number of nonwhites and attempted to deport them, but with little success. For one thing, the workers were often better off in Panama than in their countries of origin, even unemployed. Further, the canal administrators preferred to have a labor reserve from which to recruit new workers, and so they did little to help. To this day some Panamanians blame the United States for the huge injection of nonwhite and non-Latin population that has been resistant to assimilation.

The Canal Zone labor regime proved even more objectionable to Panamanians. Administrators adopted the railroad's practice of paying U.S. and European employees in gold currency and all others in Panamanian silver pesos, worth thirty-five cents. This soon evolved into a two-tiered payroll system in which U.S. whites were classified in the "gold roll" and received generous wages and benefits, becoming in effect a labor aristocracy. All others fell into the "silver roll," with its lower pay and limited benefits.[26] The system quickly became a means of racial segregation as well, wherein gold meant white and silver nonwhite. Everything from commissaries to drinking fountains existed in duplicate for the two rolls. Itinerant writer Harry Franck, who worked in the zone, described it thus: "The ICC has very dexterously dodged the necessity of lining the Zone with the offensive signs 'Black' and 'White.' 'Twould not be exactly the distinction desired anyway. Hence the line has been drawn between 'Gold' and 'Silver' employees."[27] Thus Jim Crow segregation was transplanted to Panama.

Panamanians objected to the gold and silver system for the entire life of the 1903 treaty. They decried the low pay and benefits, as well as the discriminatory treatment they received. They also resented being classified as black and having to use segregated facilities. Most strenuously, they opposed the importation of foreign laborers (largely West Indians) who competed with the natives and divided the work force according to ethnicity, nationality, race, language, and religion. Because of this "third country labor system," canal administrators were able to prevent effective unionization of the silver workers until 1946.

## Private Investment

While the canal dominated U.S.-Panamanian relations in the construction era, some American investors set up businesses in the isthmus. The U.S. government (in Washington as well as the Canal Zone) generally supported these citizens, as it did elsewhere during the age of Dollar Diplomacy. Those who established businesses in the zone itself provided goods and services primarily to American customers. Some, however, were able to form alliances with Panamanian businessmen and to move into the republic. There they competed with companies of native and foreign (mostly British) ownership. These economic ties, while unobtrusive, proved influential in relations between the two countries.

Banana cultivation attracted the largest U.S. investments in Panama during the construction era. In the 1880s and 1890s Minor C. Keith had pioneered the business along the Mosquito Coast, culminating in his incorporation of a vertically integrated operation in 1899, the United Fruit Company (UFCO). Keith's company expanded greatly in the Bocas del Toro region of northwest Panama in the early years of this century. Until World War I, Panama accounted for about 10 percent of Western Hemisphere exports of bananas. UFCO grew only about a quarter of the bananas it shipped from Panama, purchasing the bulk from private growers. Colón and Bocas del Toro provinces were the major sources.

After the war, however, a leaf blight called the Panama disease swept through the plantations and ruined production, causing UFCO to seek out uninfected lands. Panama's government opened up the Pacific slope province of Chiriqui to UFCO bananas, and in the late 1920s it virtually replaced shipments from the Bocas region. Here, however, all the bananas were raised on company land. As late as 1972 Chiriqui bananas made up over half of Panama's exports.[28]

Apart from banana plantations and firms located in the Canal Zone and the terminal cities, there was little other U.S. investment in Panama prior to 1920. Some speculators bought up concessions and land for sugar, but most did not prosper. There were also a number of failed mining ventures. Exports of fine hardwoods continued briskly until the Depression. In 1920 U.S. citizens probably held about $10 million direct investments and several million dollars in government bonds. By comparison, British investments were probably half that amount.[29]

The United States was far and away Panama's largest trade partner, buying and selling over 90 percent of the country's exports and imports.

Two parallel governments arose in Panama following independence, one for the republic (under the explicit protection of the United States) and another for the Canal Zone. Panama had the trappings of a nation-state, though the lack of a military and severely restricted financial powers made it a dependency of the United States. The Panamanian authorities cooperated with their canal superiors to facilitate construction and accepted the paternalistic guidance of U.S. officials, though not always gladly.

The Canal Zone became a military-civilian hybrid under the line authority of the secretary of war. Other services and branches of government came to play important parts in zone administration, but always under the supervision of the war secretary. The State Department found itself largely marginal in dealings between the two countries. Canal governors reigned supreme on the isthmus, far more powerful than Panama's presidents. One British minister in Panama, a long-time resident, wrote: "It is really farcical to talk of Panama as an independent state. It is really simply an annex of the Canal Zone." [30]

U.S. objectives in the republic altered during the construction era. At first, the ICC managers wished simply to build their canal with as little interference from Panama as possible. Political instability in the republic induced U.S. authorities to increase their involvement, going from tutelage, to election supervision, to policy dictation, to military protection and occupation. According to one author, "the Wilson administration tended to act as though Panama were an integral part of the United States." [31] By the time World War I ended, the canal had been open for four years and Panama was firmly under U.S. control.

Most elite Panamanians came to accept U.S. tutelage, for it offered real benefits. The military protection and intervention power meant that Panamanians "valiantly renounced the right to kill one another," according to one politician. [32] What was more, to the ambitious the construction work and the influx of perhaps two hundred thousand laborers and dependents offered great opportunities to become wealthy in business. A limited number of Panamanians secured appointments on the canal's coveted gold roll, as a U.S. goodwill gesture. Additionally, a person who cultivated the friendship of zone authorities could expect to rise in politics. President Porras even termed the Panamanian embassy in Washington the "stage upon which Panama's presidents were made." In general, success with the Americans required a person to be white or near-white, to belong to the middle or upper class, to be educated beyond high school, to have resided abroad, to speak English, to defer to foreigners, to have good family connections, and to eschew violence. Persons with these qualifications prospered during and after the construction era.

This is not to say that the United States allied with a single elite, for Panama did not have an oligarchy as such. In the 1970s strongman Omar Torrijos would say, "I did not have to deal . . . with a 400-year-old oligarchy. . . . Here the roots are more superficial."[33] Instead, two elites (or conglomerations of families) existed, one from the interior and another based in Panama City. The former was of older lineage, white, Catholic, conservative in social and political preferences, and oriented to the land and things it produced. The latter arose in the nineteenth century, had Jewish and nonwhite members who were not religious, and was cosmopolitan and more liberal in outlook. The urban elite logically viewed trade and services as the natural source of wealth in the country.[34]

These elites were further divided by political splits (as witnessed in the War of a Thousand Days) and personal feuds. Because of this, talented and savvy leaders from the middle sectors could rise in politics or the military and exercise great power. Doing so admitted them and their families to the elite, which was symbolized by membership in the Union Club, an exclusive association with headquarters in the old section of the capital. The United States usually allied with (and helped elect) those persons thought to be most capable of furthering U.S. interests, regardless of their social provenance. And the canal always stood at the center of U.S. interests in Panama.

The canal always meant more than shortened maritime routes. In the eyes of Roosevelt, Hay, Bunau-Varilla, and the American public in general, the canal symbolized the rise of the United States to great power status. It enhanced U.S. commercial and naval projection in the hemisphere; it demonstrated U.S. engineering and industrial capabilities; it showed the United States to be a country on the make, willing to act quickly and efficiently to achieve its goals; and above all it gave the United States an extraterritorial military base in a prime strategic location. From then on the United States became the dominant power in the Caribbean basin, which for all intents and purposes became an American Mediterranean. In this sense, the canal became an emblem of U.S. imperialism.

Yet paradoxically, the United States did not become an imperial power in the traditional sense nor Panama a "banana republic." World War I, which marked the high tide of western imperialism, also saw the United States eschew further territorial acquisition. For some time the State Department had attempted to obtain an inter-American treaty to prevent wars of conquest. The United States declined to keep Cuba after the Spanish-American War and eventually pulled out of the Philippines. The anti-imperialists in Congress hammered away on issues too troubling to be ignored by the expansionists: self-determination and sovereignty. Although they rarely won a vote, they eventually took the victory. It may be argued that U.S. imperialism evolved into economic domination, but territorial expansion ended in World War I.

In the words of a staunch U.S. critic of Roosevelt's gunboat diplomacy, "The tragic thing for us and for the world is that for so many years after the imperial impulse had subsided the general drift of our foreign relationships was counter to the real course of our historical and psychological evolution."[35] The canal became an outpost of the American empire that had stopped growing in the 1910s. The professional diplomats recognized the inconsistency and tried to correct our posture in Panama, but too many persons had come to accept the necessity of an American canal and a Caribbean military presence.

Despite the often demeaning treatment it received at the hands of the United States, Panama was not a mere client state. The relationship with the colossus, though highly unequal, was too visible to American and international public opinion for that. Panamanian diplomats and politicians in general developed a talent for embarrassing the United States before world organizations, beginning in the League of Nations after 1919 and continuing in the United Nations in the 1970s.[36] And the State Department, by attempting to uphold a dignified position and a modicum of legality, often served as an advocate of Panamanian interests in the U.S. government. For example, U.S. investors in Panama could not count on automatic support for their positions, nor could they operate as freely as did U.S. firms in other Central American and Caribbean countries.

# 5     From Gunboats to the Nuclear Age, 1920–1945

Jackhammers rattled through the night. Huge cranes swung tons of gravel effortlessly through the air. Money flowed freely in Panama's boom economy, and thousands of Jamaicans and other immigrants arrived. Uncle Sam was at it again, remodeling the Panama Canal so that it could transit the huge battleships and carriers the U.S. Navy was now building. The third locks project, begun in 1939, promised to restore the canal to its premier status as a strategic military bridge between the oceans. In 1942, however, the work was canceled and the boom subsided. From that point on, the canal began to recede in importance, for both the United States and Panama. Increasing numbers of ships would be unable to use the canal due to its narrow locks. Military planners acknowledged that the canal could not be protected against an all-out attack, especially against nuclear weapons. Yet at the time, few recognized how important the abandonment of the third locks project would be in the long run.

## The Troubled Twenties

U.S.-Panamanian relations settled into a pattern during the 1920s and 1930s. The United States put the finishing touches on its micro-state in the Canal Zone while making some attempts to accommodate Panama's demands for a greater share of the rewards from canal business. Panamanians pressured the United States and made symbolic attacks on the colossus, but with scant success. A more important shift came in the mid-1930s, when President Franklin Roosevelt agreed to negotiate changes in the 1903 treaty. The protectorate was formally ended but in fact remained in effect. Defense requirements and wartime mobilization led to new demands that Panama give priority to the national interests of the United States. World War II saw the high tide of U.S. impositions on Panama but also the beginning of the ebb.

The governments of the two Panamas—the Republic and the Canal Zone—stabilized after the close of World War I, and relations between them consisted of unsuccessful treaty negotiations, punctuated with desultory exchanges of accusations and denials. Belisario Porras, who had dominated the country in and out of the presidency since 1912, remained powerful through the 1920s. Porras had good anti-American credentials, having opposed independence at the hands of the United States and the treaty of 1903, but he also favored the order and progress that decent relations with the colossus could bring. In a moment of unfortunate candor, Porras even said that Panama existed "because of and for the canal."[1] His hand-picked successor, Rodolfo Chiari, continued his policy of peaceful coexistence while also promoting foreign investment and private enterprise.

The Canal Zone remained a mixed civilian-military compound loosely supervised by the secretary of war, who occasionally sought the president's approval for major decisions. About 2,000 white American supervisors and tradesmen on the gold roll managed the canal, while some seventy-six hundred West Indian blacks and Panamanians on the silver roll performed the necessary manual labor. The governor, as would become tradition, was a senior officer in the Army Corps of Engineers, promoted from chief of maintenance. It would soon become clear that the State Department had very little influence over the canal and its relationship with Panama.

Power emanated from the imposing Canal Zone administration building atop a hill in Balboa Heights. There the governor set policy for his enterprise and for the republic as well. Twice during the 1920s, at the request of two presidents, he sent troops into Panama to disperse protesters. These were mild affairs, however, compared to earlier interventions, and Americans no longer supervised Panama's elections. Usually the mere threat of intervention produced the desired behavior in Panama, as in the case of a major canal strike in 1920. When the strikers organized their pickets and held demonstrations in Panama City and Colón, the governor forced the president to ban such meetings under threat of military occupation.[2]

A number of issues soured relations between the two countries during the 1920s. First, there were housekeeping problems: tenements owned by the railroad in the terminal cities; access to the ports; commissary sales to nonemployees of the canal; water rates; and land for a cemetery in Colón. President Porras requested a new or revised treaty to settle such issues and suggested international arbitration of differences, but the United States demurred.[3] The eminent domain issue was troubling, since the 1903 treaty allowed the United States to take over land in the terminal cities it deemed "necessary and convenient." In addition, other lands needed for the maintenance or defense of the canal could be annexed by the United States. Public anger over American demands to turn most of Taboga Island into a military base had flared up in May 1920 during a ceremonial visit by General John J. Pershing. Acting President Ernesto LeFevre declared that he would not give up "another inch of national territory." This time the United States backed down.

A brief war with Costa Rica over a swath of borderland on the Pacific slope revealed how Panama's sovereignty depended on the United States. The disputed territory had been awarded to Costa Rica by a U.S. mediator in 1914, but Panama had not accepted the decision. In 1921 Costa Rican troops (aided by the United Fruit Company) seized the lands. Although the Panamanians dislodged them temporarily, they ultimately had to accept the loss when a shipload of U.S. Marines landed to secure the territory for Costa Rica.[4]

In 1923 the U.S. Congress abrogated the Taft Agreement, so the two countries signed a replacement in 1926, named the Kellogg-Alfaro Treaty after its chief negotiators. The protectorate status would continue, and Panama would automatically declare war on U.S. enemies; the canal could operate bonded warehouses but would only sell to bona fide employees; no new businesses could be formed in the zone; and a residential area in Colón owned by the railroad would be ceded to the zone. However, public opinion in Panama had become aroused by nationalist politicians, especially those belonging to a secret group called Acción Comunal. Because of the lopsided benefits the treaty gave to the United States, it was rejected by the Panamanian legislature.[5]

The 1926 treaty rejection was not too damaging to relations because the Taft Agreement remained in effect unofficially. But it did alter tradition by demonstrating that nationalist opinion in Panama had become a force to be reckoned with. It also revealed internal disputes on the U.S. side. Behind the scenes, the State Department endeavored to mend relations with Panama to the extent that Congress would allow, but canal administrators and the War Department fought to retain and expand their freedom of operation in the zone. These positions would remain fairly consistent for the next half-century.[6]

Trouble broke out in an unexpected quarter in 1925, in the bizarre Tule Revolt among the Kuna Indians of the San Blas Islands. Living isolated on a coral archipelago along the northeast coast, these tribal people had for generations remained aloof from political events in Colombia and Panama. Since 1915 they had allowed a small number of Panamanian officials to reside there as a token of allegiance to the republic. When the government attempted to force Western culture on the Indians, however, they rebelled and killed several policemen.

The U.S. government was drawn into the fray when it learned that former chargé Richard Marsh had abetted the revolt and even drafted a declaration of independence for the Kuna. A mixed U.S.-Panamanian delegation aboard a navy cruiser managed to settle the problems, and Marsh was spirited away. The Kuna have enjoyed a peaceful and autonomous existence under Panama's jurisdiction ever since.[7]

Labor affairs in the 1920s became an important issue on U.S.-Panamanian agendas, where they remained for another generation. The permanent work force inevitably attracted the notice of union organizers. Samuel Gompers, whose American Federation of Labor (AFL) represented the gold roll unions, visited Panama for over a week in early 1924 and held talks with many leaders and the canal administrators regarding reductions in force and attempts to replace Americans with silver roll employees. Meanwhile, several Panamanian labor federations had formed and made tentative contacts in the Canal Zone, usually meeting hostility from the AFL leadership.[8] The canal management succeeded in confining unionization to the gold roll.

The government of Panama in this era encouraged affiliation of silver workers with AFL unions, despite the latter's reluctance to take nonwhite members. In fact, Panamanian elites were of several minds regarding the silver roll workers. On the one hand, they wanted jobs for native workers and would have been happy to lay off and even deport West Indians to get them. And they wanted the canal to pay better wages to Panamanian employees. On the other hand, their businesses depended on West Indian customers and hence suffered during layoffs and wage reductions. Employers in Panama generally preferred having a low scale in the Canal Zone so that they would not have to pay high wages. As a result, the government of Panama did little but complain about the large numbers of unemployed West Indians in the terminal cities, about racial discrimination, and about the need for more white collar jobs for Panamanians. Unfortunately for the West Indians and their children, naturalization legislation left them in limbo regarding citizenship, and their community began to build up its own institutions for survival and protection. These included schools, churches, mutual aid societies, professional groups, and sports clubs.

The 1920s saw some improvements in economic relations between Panama and the United States. Canal Zone procurement officers began buying some staples from Panamanian producers, helping to spread around the profits. The beef contract, in particular, benefited wealthy ranchers in the interior. In addition, the State Department encouraged U.S. banks to make more loans to Panama, using the canal annuity payments as collateral. Some of the proceeds were employed for railroad and highway construction to transport goods to ports.

## The Depression Decade

The Great Depression affected Panama primarily through two mechanisms: Canal Zone reductions-in-force and devaluation of the

U.S. dollar that slashed the value of the annuity payment by 40 percent. Large layoffs in 1930 and 1931 were made as part of the U.S. government economy program, and they affected both purchases of commodities and employment. Several thousand silver roll workers swelled the ranks of unemployed in the terminal cities, and wages were cut across the board. The fact that most of the unemployed were West Indians or their descendants led to a clamor for their repatriation: the Panamanian government insisted that the United States pay for returning unemployed West Indians to their islands of origin.[9]

In early January 1931 Acción Comunal, the secret political organization instrumental in rejecting the 1926 treaty, deposed the existing government and installed one of its sympathizers as provisional president. This coup would affect U.S.-Panamanian relations for a long time to come. Acción Comunal was a nationalist pressure group whose members sought to reduce U.S. influence in their country and to garner more benefits for their people. Their slogan, "Panama for the Panamanians," conveyed the spirit of chauvinism that appealed to the public and that swept into the presidency in the early 1930s. The government would henceforth put renewed pressure on the United States to share more of the profits from the canal with Panama.

The U.S. government refrained from involvement in the coup, signaling its intention no longer to prevent revolutions in Panama but merely to assure that no politician threatened the canal or U.S. vital interests. This change was in keeping with the abandonment of the Roosevelt Corollary during the tenure of Henry Stimson as secretary of state. Stimson recognized that military occupation and constant intervention in the internal affairs of many smaller Caribbean basin countries probably undermined U.S. influence in the region.[10]

Two willful and ambitious brothers came to dominate Panamanian politics in the 1930s, Harmodio and Arnulfo Arias Madrid, leaders in the Acción Comunal coup. They deeply altered relations with the United States as well. The Arias brothers came from a rural lower-middle-class family in the interior of the country and had no blood links to the traditional Arias clan. Both received advanced degrees abroad, Harmodio in law and economics in England and Arnulfo in medicine in the United States. Harmodio, the elder, formed a

thriving law firm that represented corporate clients in Panama and
wealthy Panamanians in the Canal Zone. He also served in the legislature during the 1920s, acting as a spokesman for Acción Comunal.
Arnulfo practiced public medicine during the 1920s. Despite the fact
that he was only recruited to the Acción Comunal coup in late 1930 he
emerged as its most forceful and daring leader.

After Harmodio won election as president in 1932 for a four-year
term, he set out to wrest canal concessions from the United States. He
made a surprise visit to Washington in October 1933 to appeal directly
to President Franklin Roosevelt for help. The latter, in the spirit of the
Good Neighbor policy, agreed to curb many canal practices that Panamanians found damaging to their interests, especially with regard to
commissary and restaurant sales to noncanal employees and repatriation of retired West Indians. After the talks, Roosevelt said at a news
conference, Arias's "visit does illustrate the practical way of taking up
problems that occur between different countries." [11]

These and other measures did not provide sufficient relief, however, and in early 1934 negotiations began for a modification of the
1903 treaty. Roosevelt played an important part in the talks, during
which he even made a visit to Panama.[12]

The 1936 treaty negotiations were in a sense a continuation of those
of 1924 to 1926 (which in turn sought to prolong elements of the
Taft Agreement), though the emphases were altered by new circumstances. Panama was more than ever determined to increase its share
of business generated by the canal, improve Panamanian canal employees' wages and benefits, raise the annuity to offset the dollar
devaluation, and end the U.S. right to land acquisition. U.S. negotiators focused on security, especially the right to appropriate lands
for defense purposes in an emergency. The American residents of the
zone—called Zonians—were a powerful lobbying group, however,
that sought to protect their community's special privileges.[13] As had
become standard practice, the canal authorities, backed by the War
Department, fought against most concessions, while the Department
of State (with White House support) favored ceding in nonstrategic
areas in order to promote better relations with Panama and Latin
America.

The treaty, sixteen accompanying notes, and three separate conventions signed in early 1936 went beyond the 1926 treaty and were well received by the Panamanians. The main elements of the package were elimination of the protectorate status of Panama, increase in the annuity to $430,000, the end of the right to acquire land, promises to limit commissary and PX sales to canal personnel, authorization for Panama to operate radio stations (banned since World War I), and promises of equal treatment of U.S. and Panamanian employees. Some elements of the new treaty went into effect in mid-1936 without awaiting ratification.

The U.S. Senate, however, was not enthusiastic about signing away what the War Department claimed were strategic U.S. interests, especially with tensions rising in Europe, and it did not approve the treaty until 1939.[14] In addition, Roosevelt had damaged relations with Congress by attempting to pack the Supreme Court to get his way with legislation. So the Senate only ratified the treaty upon the insistence of the White House that it was essential prior to a meeting of foreign ministers in Panama to plan for hemispheric defense.

The rise of aggressive new leadership in Panama and the U.S. policy to tolerate any regime that did not threaten its interests inevitably gave the National Police a larger role in the political arena. Much of the electorate no longer expected or even wanted members of the old elites to lead the country, because they were associated with the hated 1903 treaty. The United States would not send troops to supervise elections or to "teach democracy." Accordingly, the Arias brothers and their allies strengthened the National Police and used it to rig elections and intimidate the opposition. The escalating use of force and high political stakes created a strong rivalry between the Ariases, however, further destabilizing relations with the United States.

The 1940 presidential contest saw especially crude use of violence on the part of the government. Within a year the police (encouraged by the opposition and by Harmodio) overthrew Arnulfo, in part because he had set up a secret police as a rival force. By late 1943 a U.S. intelligence summary of political trends in Panama would begin, "Whoever controls the Policía Nacional writes Panama's political history."[15] For a time the United States could ignore the resultant instability, but in the long run the elites of both countries would have to grapple with a military force of their own creation.

## World War II

After the start of the war in Europe, the Panamanian government hosted a consultation of foreign ministers in September 1939. Its purpose was to plan ways to guarantee the neutrality of the hemisphere in the conflict and to reduce its negative impact on their economies. Roosevelt had used the meeting to pressure the Senate into approving the 1936 treaty, arguing that Panama was the focal point of the U.S. naval empire in the Caribbean and a crucial link in its international defense strategy.[16] Panama in the meantime cooperated with U.S. authorities to place Axis citizens under surveillance and to prevent their threatening the security of the canal.

The cooperative relationship between the United States and Panama regarding defense preparations ended in mid-1940, however, after the election of Arnulfo Arias as president for a four-year term. Arias took an intensely nationalistic stance by demanding that the United States pay handsomely for any lands leased for military purposes. He also kept Panama strictly neutral by prohibiting propaganda of Allied as well as Axis agents and by refusing to arm Panamanian flag vessels. The U.S. intelligence community there came to regard Arias as untrustworthy because of his travels in Italy and Germany during the 1930s and his associations with pro-Axis individuals. The dilatory defense sites negotiations strengthened these convictions. Even State Department officials sympathetic to Panama's interests believed that Arias's demands were excessive.[17]

Arnulfo Arias was an exalted figure during his first presidency (1940–41), extremely active and willful. He had overseen drafting and promulgation of a new, nationalistic constitution that sought to expand the role of government in civil society and to strengthen and centralize administration. He introduced a number of bills and decrees enforcing a regimentation on the traditionally relaxed populace.

Among the most controversial measures were those directed against West Indians and their descendants, whose citizenship, businesses, jobs, and civil rights were put in jeopardy. For these and other reasons, a good deal of domestic opposition to Arias arose during 1941, including that of his own brother and former president, Harmodio.[18]

During the president's unauthorized absence from the country early in October 1941, his minister of justice, Ricardo Adolfo de la Guardia, deposed him and assumed the presidency. U.S. intelligence agents had informed de la Guardia of Arnulfo's trip and encouraged the coup but were probably not otherwise involved. The new president, a political moderate, adopted a policy of collaboration with U.S. military planners, and by mid-1942 he approved a defense sites agreement that met U.S. needs. In exchange, however, he exacted a dozen concessions with major financial commitments that the United States had not accepted before Pearl Harbor.[19]

Upon the U.S. entry into the war in December 1941, U.S. and Panamanian officials moved quickly to secure the canal. President de la Guardia declared war on the Axis countries, which led to the departure of their embassy personnel. Over the next several months authorities detained over twelve hundred citizens of the Axis nations. After screening, most were released, but 327 persons suspected of espionage were deported to internment camps in the United States. The U.S. and Panamanian governments also instituted postal censorship, civil defense measures, and strict surveillance of the airspace around the canal. These moves virtually eliminated Axis intelligence activities in Panama.[20] Tight security was prompted by the fact that the canal was highly vulnerable to enemy attack. As it turned out, though, only one serious Axis plan ever existed for a major assault on the canal, and it was canceled.[21]

The war did have a major impact on Panama's economy, however, much more than the previous conflict. This was due to additional highway construction, work on a third set of canal locks and other defense projects, and increased purchases for troop and ship supply. The road jobs consisted of a stretch from Panama City to the U.S. base at Rio Hato along the route of the Pan-American Highway and another between Panama City and Colón, the Transístmica. These works, along with the third locks expansion, led to the importation of twenty-two thousand workers from Central America and the West Indies and enormous purchases of food and materials of all sorts. The resultant expenditures caused an economic boom in Panama nearly as large as the original construction project.[22]

The wartime prosperity raised hopes for permanent improvements in relations between Panama and the United States. New businesses began to supply building materials and food for the zone. Many well-to-do Panamanians received appointments on the gold roll and enjoyed special status in the zone. The twelve-point agreement of 1942 promised to improve transportation and create new business opportunities in Panama. In 1942 the U.S.-sponsored Institute of Inter-American Affairs became the first agency to promote economic development in Panama, relying on increased sales to the Canal Zone. So despite the disruptions due to the war and emergency controls they necessitated, Panamanians were optimistic about continued economic development after 1945.

The Panamanian government also helped to promote academic exchanges through the establishment of the Inter-American University in the capital. First proposed in 1913, the university was finally created in 1943 as an educational branch of the Pan-American Union. Since it had no buildings, it occupied the premises of the University of Panama. During and after the war several U.S. professors taught there, which improved intellectual ties between the two countries and led to several fine publications. In 1946, however, it lapsed due to funding cuts.[23]

In the last year of the war, Panamanian leaders made a concerted effort to assure that the country would not be returned to the subordinate status it had suffered during the first three decades of its existence. Organized labor made the first approaches. A West Indian union leader visited with Vice-President Henry Wallace during a visit to the Canal Zone in early 1943, requesting improved treatment of silver workers. A Latin-Panamanian group also approached Wallace and later Eleanor Roosevelt to petition for more gold roll jobs for their members. They also asked Mexican labor leader Vicente Lombardo

Toledano to carry to Washington their request that the U.S. government end racial discrimination in canal employment.

The Roosevelt administration, committed to lessening racial discrimination at home, proved sensitive to these pressures. When word of these complaints reached the White House in early 1944, Roosevelt had an aide draft a letter to the governor of the Canal Zone urging him to act fairly and in the spirit of the Good Neighbor policy. Yet the president refrained from ordering an overhaul of the canal labor system. Presumably winning the war demanded all his attention. By now, however, the Panamanian government lent its support to the campaign by bringing up canal labor grievances at the May 1944 International Labor Organization (ILO) meeting in Philadelphia. This threatened to embarrass the United States at a time when the administration was poised to assume leadership of the Western world through the formation of the United Nations. The ILO charges produced a request that the Canal Zone be included in a survey of dependent territories, but little else. Such efforts would, however, bear fruit after the war.[24]

An important change had occurred in the Panamanian position toward the silver workers on the canal that would alter the relationship with the United States in later decades. Until the 1940s, most Panamanians regarded the West Indians and their descendants as unwanted aliens. This had allowed the canal administrators to exploit them as third-country nationals, to keep Panamanian employees in inferior positions, and to avoid compliance with the 1936 promise of equal treatment. By 1945, however, Panama recognized the citizenship rights of all descendants born there and rushed through naturalization papers for immigrants. As one foreign minister remarked, racial discrimination toward the silver workers in the Canal Zone, the U.S. Achilles heel in its relations with Panama, constituted Panama's most powerful opportunity to force change in the Canal Zone. But to use it Panama had to defend all silver workers, regardless of ethnic origin.

As far as many Panamanians were concerned, Franklin Roosevelt's Good Neighbor policy had been little more than a public relations ploy. The New Deal turned out to be a raw deal. True, the 1936 treaty and associated agreements codified understandings reached in earlier decades, and the annuity increase helped offset Panama's perennial trade deficit. Yet so many measures went unenforced that Panamanians could hardly be happy with their status by the end of the war. The gold and silver rolls, with their grossly disparate wages and benefits, correlated almost exactly with U.S. and Panamanian citizenship and nearly as closely with the color line. Thus Panamanians were treated as inferior workers and visitors in lands nominally theirs. The commissaries, PXs, clubhouses, and other facilities in the zone supplied all manner of goods to Panamanians who could afford them, to the detriment of local businesses. Until 1939 the United States could claim virtually any land it wished by asserting that it was necessary for canal defense. Panama was still a protectorate but enjoyed few benefits from that status.

Each branch of the U.S. government viewed Panama a little differently. The Pentagon saw Panama as a foreign country in a strategic location where military bases could maintain a U.S. presence in the hemisphere at relatively little cost. The fact that they were near the Panama Canal was fortuitous but hardly necessary. The State Department regarded Panama as a remnant of an imperialist age when heads of powerful states could create and extinguish countries at will. The unequal treatment afforded Panamanians was an embarrassment and a hindrance to better relations with Latin America as a whole. The Department of Commerce viewed Panama as an international shipping utility and insisted that it benefit U.S. and world commerce. U.S. presidents often had trouble deciding upon which role the canal played and hence deferred major decisions put to them.

The American public, meanwhile, had been raised on stories of the legendary conquest of the jungles at Panama and of the heroic job of building the canal. They had come to regard the canal as an outpost of empire, a monument to American engineering, and an act of benevolence toward the rest of the world—"pro mundi beneficio." The nearly sacred status Americans accorded to the canal made any change there doubly hard to accomplish.

Panamanians, of course, saw the canal in completely different ways.

They were proud of its operation, to be sure, but they were no longer awed by the machinery and ship operations. Instead they felt betrayed because it benefited them so little. They had dreamed of becoming a modern, prosperous nation due to the canal, but they saw that those improvements were limited to the American sector. They regarded the canal as an El Dorado that could still pay for modernizing their country if its profits were invested there.

Perhaps most galling of all was the disparity, the stark contrast between living conditions in the zone and in Panama. The former displayed its neatly painted, landscaped buildings patrolled by intimidating policemen, where white Americans lived in a comfort they could not have afforded at home. The stores and warehouses seemed ready to burst with the latest luxury goods from the United States at prices far below those in Panama. In the republic, by contrast, the zone was bordered by squalor: aged wooden tenements, tawdry nightclubs and brothels, trinket shops, and unkempt jungle. It was a disparity that all visitors noticed and remarked upon and caused Panamanians to feel a deep sense of injustice.

Just as the suspension of the third locks project eventually led to a U.S. reassessment of the strategic importance of the Panama Canal, the end of the war caused Panamanians to launch a campaign to increase their benefits from the ship operation. And for almost the first time in the history of the two countries' relations, Panama seemed to have the advantage on the colossus.

# 6    Uneasy Partners, 1945–1960

Toward the end of the war, the head of the Caribbean Command, in charge of all military bases in the Canal Zone, put to paper some thoughts on the growing nationalism of Panamanians and their demands to share in the profits from the canal and transit business. He cited as evidence the formation of the Panamanian Merchants' and Industrialists' Association in 1943 for the purpose of reserving business for natives, the 1944 immigration exclusion of Africans and Asians, the foreign minister's demand that Panama control commercial aviation on the isthmus and that the zone end commissary sales to nonemployees, newspaper articles decrying U.S. military infringement of Panama's sovereignty, the continued attraction of a Hispanidad movement like that in Franco's Spain, and a desire to eliminate U.S. influence in general. He noted that some radicals went to the "extreme of striving for the eventual control and operation of the canal itself." Later he commented on an impending visit to Washington by the foreign minister. He expected complaints about a number of items, among them unequal treatment of U.S. and Panamanian canal employees; housing shortages; U.S. operation of Panama's water and sewage systems; the need for an international airport; and a lack of highways into agricultural regions. In short, a whole range of issues surfaced by 1945 that were pursued aggressively by the Panamanian government. U.S. officials girded themselves to resist such pressures.[1]

Several trends coincided to bring so many problems to a head simultaneously in 1945. The war had postponed attention to certain grievances, causing them to accumulate. In particular, many promises in the 1936 treaty and 1942 twelve-points agreements now fell due. U.S. government policies toward race relations at home (for example, the banning of job discrimination by race and the decision to integrate the armed services) also made it appear that the Canal Zone might be desegregated. The U.S. sponsorship of the United Nations, where member states were juridically equal, suggested that the U.S.-Panamanian relationship might become more equitable. Finally, as one observer wrote, "The ephemeral character of the American empire has led to a certain looseness and vacillation in American policy." So as the world adjusted to peace in 1945, Panamanian leaders prepared for some tough bargaining with U.S. representatives.[2]

## Canal Zone Labor Reforms

Labor relations in the Canal Zone topped Panama's list of issues in 1945. The Panamanian case was simple. Growth of population and improvements in schooling in the republic meant that many more citizens were qualified for skilled jobs on the canal. The Canal Zone payroll of $32 million made a substantial contribution to national income; therefore, increased employment and higher wages would pump up the economy immediately. An auxiliary note to the 1936 treaty signed by Cordell Hull and Ricardo Alfaro promised equal employment opportunities and treatment for citizens of the two countries, but it had not been implemented. So Panama pressed hard for its enforcement.

Simultaneously the silver roll canal workers finally unionized, with the reluctant approval of management. A new generation of leaders had emerged in the West Indian community, persons born on the isthmus and determined to fight for better wages and benefits. They knew enough about the U.S. system to use its constitutional principles against the de facto segregation in which they lived and worked. They formed a Canal Zone chapter (Local 713) of the United Public Workers of America (UPW) and immediately received help from its U.S. headquarters in setting up offices and recruiting membership. The canal administration, meanwhile, accepted the new arrangements because of fears that a more militant, leftist union might be formed. Since the 1944 appeals to the White House and the ILO, Mexican labor leader Vicente Lombardo Toledano had shown an interest in establishing a Panamanian chapter of his Latin American Confederation of Labor

(CTAL). Local 713 was seen as the lesser of two evils. Its leaders were cautioned, however, against any dealings with Panamanian officials—it was to be strictly a Canal Zone union abiding by the rules of U.S.-style unionism.[3]

Local 713, backed by the Panamanian government and the UPW headquarters, did achieve some advances in wages and working conditions for silver canal employees in the late 1940s. The labels *gold* and *silver* were changed to *U.S. rate* and *local rate,* and signs on segregated facilities were removed. The Canal Zone governor, Joseph Mehaffey, had spent many years in Panama and genuinely wished to improve labor and race relations there, if it could be done without disrupting his principal job, "to get ships through the canal economically and efficiently."

The cold war erupted in the late 1940s, however, and endangered the tentative advances made by Local 713. The UPW came under attack in the United States for being too leftist or even communist, a charge that tainted Local 713.[4] The conservative American Federation of Labor (AFL) set out to take over international representation of public employees, embarking on a member raid on the Congress of Industrial Organizations (CIO), to which UPW belonged. These two behemoths also fought for the right to represent Latin American unions, for it meant subsidies from the U.S. government under the Point IV program. In late 1949 the AFL emerged the victor and set up a rival public employees union. It also won the right to represent Latin American unions in general.

Within months Local 713 closed down. It was not replaced by an AFL affiliate, however, because the AFL had always represented the U.S.-rate unions and was thus anathema to the local-rate leaders. Instead, they formed a new CIO-affiliated group, Local 900. The new local rate union did not fare any better than its predecessor, however, because of budgetary cutbacks imposed by Washington after 1950. When its leaders became more militant in their demands and allied themselves with the Panamanian government, they suffered retaliation from management and nearly folded.

## U.S. Reappraisal of the Canal
## and the 1947 Treaty

Efforts to defend the canal during World War II and the advent of atomic weapons in 1945 caused U.S. strategic planners to attempt to preserve the wartime defense complex in Panama.[5] On the one hand, to guard against air raids—to which the canal was eminently vulnerable—the military established no fewer than 134 observation and antiaircraft sites throughout Panama. In addition, authorities jailed citizens of the Axis powers who might have sabotaged the canal. Such efforts, customary in conventional war, could not protect the canal from attack with an atomic weapon. Only a permanent network of outlying bases from which approaching aircraft could be interdicted would provide an effective defense for the canal. Thus the Pentagon insisted on retaining some of the bases occupied during the war so that it could continue to use the Canal Zone as a principal defense installation.

On the other hand, the military utility of the canal had long been questioned. The locks were too narrow for the navy's newest capital ships, a fact that had spurred the brief third locks project of 1939 to 1942. Even with wider locks, the canal was a bottleneck exposing ships to attack during transit. The solution, according to Governor Mehaffey, was a sea-level canal. Other plans surfaced, too, including widened locks and a new summit-level lake. Any of these projects would require expenditures in the billions of dollars. Without them, the canal and its zone would inevitably be reduced to secondary strategic importance.

In the end the cold war shifted U.S. attentions and priorities to Europe and condemned the canal to quasi-obsolescence. John Major neatly summed up the impact of the reappraisal, saying the canal "had been built to serve the purposes of a regional power with relatively limited military resources. Those days were done, and the waterway increasingly began to seem the relic of a bygone age."[6]

At this juncture, overwrought Panamanian nationalism reinforced the tendency under way in Washington. Students, politicians, diplomats, newspaper editors, and others had long demanded a larger share in the profits from the canal, and they focused on the bases negotiations to make their point. In a vehement patriotic campaign, they marshaled public opinion against the bases agreement. In December 1947 the Panamanian Assembly unanimously voted them down. Though the action hurt their short-term interests, in the long run it declared Panama's desire for a demilitarized canal.[7]

This rejection, or *rechazo* as it is called in Spanish, caused a chain reaction of events in U.S.-Panamanian relations. It prompted the Pentagon to abandon the air defense bases and to downgrade the canal in its worldwide strategic scheme. (The rising menace of communism in Europe also contributed to this decision.) It ruled out any major improvements to the canal. It made U.S. government agencies less cooperative in dealing with Panamanian agencies. Finally, it reinforced the decision made in 1951 to reorganize the canal to reduce treasury expenditures on nonmaritime activities.

Among Panamanians, however, the *rechazo* symbolized their growing assertiveness and desire to be taken seriously by U.S. authorities. It brought about national unity and solidarity, at least momentarily. It cast university students in heroic roles and the National Guard (which beat down demonstrators) in traitorous ones. And it served notice to the political elite that it would be held accountable for any concessions made to the United States. Panamanians in effect had repudiated the old relationship of subservience and forced elites to reformulate the alliance.

## Postwar Economic Relations

The Panamanian economy became sluggish in the postwar years due to a sharp drop in expenditures in the Canal Zone. The rejection of the bases agreement brought on a recession, with high levels of unemployment and fiscal distress. The situation only worsened after the 1951 reorganization. Therefore, Panamanian leaders attempted to stimulate and diversify the economy so that it would be less dependent on the canal. As usual, these efforts affected relations with the United States.

Panama made a concerted effort to develop an international airport in the late 1940s, hoping to make the country a hub of air as well as sea traffic. The site chosen was Tocumen, some fifteen miles northeast of Panama City. The facility opened for business in mid-1947, but most commercial flights continued to use Albrook Field in the Canal Zone. In 1948 the two countries began negotiating an agreement to transfer all civilian traffic to Tocumen in order to restrict Albrook to military use and to alleviate congestion there. All commercial flights would be routed to Tocumen, and Panama would exempt canal employees landing there from customs and immigration checks.

Coming as it did on the heels of the bases rejection, the air convention awoke intense interest in the press and political circles. The potential benefits to Panama were huge, since Tocumen could become a major provider of aviation services. Moreover, business would be transferred from the zone to Panama. Thus the government approved the agreement in early 1949, and the Assembly ratified it shortly afterward. (Few foresaw then that Tocumen would also serve as a transfer point for drug shipments.)[8]

The government also attempted to stimulate tourism by sponsoring an inter-American congress of tourism directors in 1947. The meeting was held in the recently completed luxury hotel, Hotel El Panamá, in the elegant Carmen district, to attract and serve tourists. It was designed in part to take business from the Canal Zone's Tivoli Hotel, which soon afterward suspended operations. A few years later the canal leased its hotel in Colón to Panamanian businessmen.

Another enterprise, the Colón Free Zone, began generating more income for Panama in the early 1950s. Located at the northern terminus of the canal, Colón had originally prospered because of transit business. During the 1930s, however, it suffered a decline in fortunes, and by the end of the war it was a shambles. Local and federal authorities collaborated to create a huge area for bonded warehouses and factories, where imported components could be assembled and reexported to other Latin American countries. Because the Free Zone generated employment, profits, subcontracts, and some immigration, it was deemed a major success.

Finally, representatives of the new U.S. aid program, called Point IV, and the World Bank conducted studies in Panama to find projects of economic utility. Among their priorities was completion of the Pan-American Highway from Panama City to the Costa Rican border. This could spur trade and would also link isolated producing regions with urban markets. It would be many years before the highway was completed, but this approach redirected attention from the canal to general development of the economy.[9]

In 1951 another rude shock jolted the Panamanian economy, the so-called canal reorganization. Briefly, the U.S. government altered operating procedures in the Canal Zone in such a way as to make it self-supporting, and in the next several years net expenditures dropped sharply. The decision was based in part on reports that U.S. employees in the Canal Zone (ironically referred to as Southern Comfort) enjoyed an extremely high standard of living. Critics pointed out that the zone was a perfect socialistic enterprise, with no private property and total government care for its residents.[10] The austerity measures carried out in the early 1950s hurt the Zonians, but it also had a devastating impact on Panama, deepening the postwar recession.

Several changes in canal operations proved especially damaging to Panama's economy. First, the administration reversed its policy of providing low-cost housing for noncitizen employees. Thousands of families were forced out of the zone and into the terminal cities in the mid-1950s, creating housing shortages and inflating rents. Second, social services for noncitizen employees were curtailed, and the canal began charging full tuition for nonresident children to attend school. Third, the general contraction of wages and benefits meant less money in circulation for Panamanian commerce. So the hard times began in the Canal Zone but quickly spread throughout the isthmus.

U.S. authorities attempted to ameliorate the situation, especially with the approach of Panama's presidential elections in May 1952. They feared that communism might gain more followers due to unemployment. The ambassador suggested a transfusion of money from canal contracts and expenditures into "Panama's diseased economic body." He also urged a public relations campaign to improve the perception of the canal by Panamanians and accelerated expenditures under the Point IV program. Ultimately, they hoped to achieve some degree of stability in urban areas.[11]

After 1952 government-to-government aid supplemented the canal as an external subsidy to Panama's dependent economy. The rationale was spelled out by aid specialist Vance Rogers:

> Panama's unique geographic and political relationship to the Canal Zone and the U.S. has fostered problems of an economic, political and social nature. The Republic's traditional role of an economic dependency of the U.S. has resulted in a hypernationalism and an ambivalent attitude toward the U.S. which more often than not is expressed by resentment and distrust. A second major problem . . . is low national productivity, which is attributable to over-dependence on activities in the Canal Zone. Developmental possibilities lie in the field of agriculture and related industrial development. Illiteracy, disease, primitive methods and the lack of transportation combine to keep the Panamanian farmer on a subsistence level, and the Republic on an import basis.[12]

This shift proved important, for the State Department, rather than the Pentagon, tended the spigot. The flow of aid increased, to an average of about $7 million per year in the 1950s. Moreover, expenditures were more closely attuned to political events than administrative concerns.

The candidate who emerged triumphant in the 1952 election, Col. José Antonio Remón, proved decisive in reshaping U.S.-Panamanian relations. Born into a middle-class family impoverished by the father's alcoholism, Remón struggled to get ahead, pushed by a forceful mother and well-to-do relatives. After working in several jobs, Remón managed to win an appointment to the military academy in Mexico. After graduating third in his class in 1931, he received a captain's commission in Panama's National Police. He found himself sidelined by the Arias brothers in the mid-1930s, however, so he operated several businesses until eventually winning reappointment to the police in 1940. He received training in the United States in 1941 and made Lieutenant Colonel that same year.

In the 1940s Remón became the sort of constabulary chief the United

States had sponsored in other Caribbean countries a decade earlier (for example, Trujillo in the Dominican Republic, Batista in Cuba, and Somoza in Nicaragua). A State Department briefing paper for President Eisenhower stated that "Remón is not well educated and lacks experience in international affairs, but is strongly anti-Communist and is considered pro–United States." He also had no qualms about using force to preserve order. As he rose through the ranks to become commander of the police in 1947, he amassed great wealth and power. He became Panama's kingmaker.[13]

Presidents entered and left as if by a revolving door during the years 1948 to 1952, mostly chosen and deposed by Remón. The instability troubled U.S. observers and stymied plans for economic development. Many came to believe that only Remón himself in the presidency could keep the government on an even keel. Thus the U.S. embassy saw his election as president in 1952 with some relief, for "the only possible hope for continuing stability in Panama lies in Colonel Remón's achieving and maintaining effective control of the Government, at least until something can be done to stimulate [economic] development."[14] Remón held a few wild cards, however.

The State Department immediately cranked up aid programs and encouraged other agencies to follow suit. Remón responded positively, setting up new agencies and revamping others to receive money and technical assistance. The justification echoed cold war fears likely to persuade both the Pentagon and Congress: if Panamanians would focus on their own development it *"would diminish vulnerabilities which are being constantly and adroitly exploited by Communist, Peronist and anti-American elements. . . . Friendly relations with the Panamanian Government are essential for the security and efficient functioning of the Canal."* This sort of rationale would be echoed in the 1960s and 1970s as well.[15]

Remón generally got good marks for his economic reforms, especially those carried out by the new Economic Development Institute (IFE) and the various *servicios* he created. The government raised taxes to generate surplus for investment, used price and tariff controls to stimulate production, obtained loans from U.S. and international agencies, shifted emphasis to agricultural pursuits, and promoted health and education programs for a more robust workforce. All these efforts received encouragement from the embassy.[16]

Another lasting change Remón made was conversion of the police into the National Guard in 1953. More than a simple name change, this move transformed the guard into a quasi-military force with a larger budget and heavier ordinance. Thereafter, the guard received regular military assistance from the United States, including officer training in the Canal Zone's School of the Americas. Thus strengthened, the guard became a major institutional actor in domestic politics.[17]

## The 1955 Treaty

Remón surprised U.S. officials by issuing a strident public appeal for new treaty negotiations. The U.S. ambassador barely concealed his anger at Remón's "blunt and crude" approach, which he regarded as demagogic.[18] It was, however, a case of the apprentice learning his lesson too well: Remón was determined to promote economic development, and he insisted that the Canal Zone make a larger contribution to that effort. In the early months of 1953 he built a nonpartisan consensus in favor of treaty talks and asked the embassy to arrange a meeting with President Eisenhower. In a March speech he coined the slogan for his campaign: "Neither charity nor millions: we want justice!" The State Department opposed the visit, but the following month Eisenhower agreed to it and treaty discussions, hoping to avoid a confrontation or a radicalization of the political climate in Panama.[19]

In August Remón took the bold step of convoking a huge rally in the capital to build public support for his negotiating team, about to leave for Washington. Perhaps one hundred thousand persons attended the meeting, called a "date with the fatherland," making this one of the greatest shows of national unity in Panama's history. A new style of diplomacy, using popular opinion and mobilization, had dawned in U.S.-Panamanian relations.

Remón's negotiators, all veteran diplomats, pushed for a long list of reforms: implementation of the equal employment promise of 1936;

the power to tax Panamanian canal employees; elimination of contraband sales; a share in canal profits; more zone purchases of local commodities; and many other items. Significantly, Remón's demands included explicit recognition of Panamanian sovereignty in the zone and equal display of the two countries' flags. This wish list would have drastically altered Canal Zone operations, and it was met with strong objections by U.S. officials in various branches, who formed an interdepartmental committee for the negotiations.[20]

The talks, which began in early September, promised to be lengthy since the Panamanian list was long and U.S. officials required time to reach decisions. Panama's team asked Remón to nudge President Eisenhower during his visit to Washington later in the month. Abandoning protocol, Remón did so in a forty-minute meeting. John Foster Dulles played the tough-guy role, while Eisenhower wished to concede where U.S. vital interests were not at stake.[21]

The negotiations continued for about a year, while Remón managed to keep public opinion inflamed. In January 1954 he held a rally to show labor union support, including that of Local 900 in the Canal Zone. In March his energetic wife, Cecilia, used the Organization of American States (OAS) meeting in Caracas to denounce racism and the "lamentable discrimination" against Panamanians in the Canal Zone, which, she believed, played into the hands of the communists. Such pressures, combined with the developing crises in Guatemala and Egypt, wrung major concessions from the United States. In Guatemala President Jacobo Arbenz was carrying out leftist reforms that threatened UFCO landholdings and other U.S. interests; in Egypt Col. Gamal Abdel Nasser had seized power in a military coup and had demanded control of the Suez Canal. The United States could ill afford another hot spot in Panama.

The treaty finally signed in January 1955 represented a major advance in comparison with accords signed in 1936 and 1942, but in hindsight it clearly conceded too little too late. Panama's gains were mostly economic: the right to tax canal employees, stricter contraband rules, an annuity of $1.93 million, return of railroad properties in Panama and Colón, a bridge over the canal, a lease for continued

U.S. use of an outlying air base (Rio Hato), and equal pay rates regardless of nationality. For its part the United States clung to the 1903 sovereignty rights and refused to give Panama a share in tolls because it would imply a parallel right to share in canal management.[22]

The treaty would soon come under fire by Panamanian nationalists, but it was easily ratified by mid-1955. Remón had been assassinated in gangland style on January 2, and the new president and Assembly, not wishing to prolong the treaty debate, rushed to approve it. Several months later the U.S. Senate followed suit. The economic benefits that it conferred on Panama were not shared equally. Canal employees—mostly descendants of the West Indians—paid a high price. They lost housing and commissary privileges and began paying income taxes. The equal pay agreement was more apparent than real. At best, according to one West Indian leader, the sacrifice proved their patriotism.[23] The treasury and business community, on the other hand, benefited the most from the treaty provisions on taxes and commissary sales.

Political and strategic arrangements changed little under the 1955 treaty. Secretary of State John Foster Dulles rejected every Panamanian effort to weaken U.S. claims to de facto sovereignty in the zone. Save for changes to the lease on Rio Hato, defense matters remained the same. In fact the Pentagon saw no need to negotiate a bases agreement—the United States had created a dozen in the Canal Zone—on the grounds that the bases were authorized under the provisions of the 1903 treaty. But Panamanians argued that most of them had little to do with defending the canal and served hemispheric strategic purposes.

In fact, the canal itself had lost most of its military value due to its narrowness and vulnerability to attack. As Larry Pippin noted, "What had been a 'vital lifeline' in 1939 was not so in 1955."[24] Yet the bases clustered in the Canal Zone provided the United States with a strategic presence in the Americas. A jungle warfare school set up during World War II trained thousands of Latin American officers in counterinsurgency; elaborate intelligence operations were based in the Canal Zone; an informal inter-American defense network ran out of the bases there; and forces could be deployed from Panama to virtually any part of the hemisphere in a short time. The Pentagon cared far more about these military assets than about the canal, yet without the canal the bases would have to be authorized by separate treaties with Panama.

## The Partnership Imperiled

In late 1956 Eisenhower learned that "before the ink was dry on these [1955] agreements, high Panamanian officials were stating publicly that [they] did not satisfy Panama's aspirations." [25] Egypt's seizure of the Suez Canal in July 1956 made the concessions wrung from the United States appear paltry indeed to Panamanians. In addition, the U.S. Congress delayed writing implementing legislation needed for the 1955 treaty—especially for the so-called single wage scale. Congressional Democrats, unhappy with the treaty, empaneled a group of experts to examine the possibility of a new canal somewhere else in Central America. The two partners drifted farther apart, and relations reached a crisis in the late 1950s. [26]

The new Panamanian president, Ernesto de la Guardia, appointed Ricardo Arias, a sharp critic of U.S. canal policy, as ambassador to Washington, and Aquilino Boyd as foreign secretary. Together they launched a campaign to expand Panama's benefits from the canal at any cost. The foreign office proposed exploiting mineral rights in the Canal Zone and a 50-50 split of toll revenues, similar to the agreement between Venezuela and the oil companies. Panama, they signaled, would no longer be satisfied with crumbs from the colossus's table. [27]

The Eisenhower administration did push through legislation for the single wage system in 1958, and the president's brother Milton made a point of meeting with President de la Guardia on his fact-finding trip through Latin America that year. De la Guardia claimed that Panama needed $40 million to get the economy moving and complained about the slow pace of treaty implementation. [28] Milton Eisenhower reported back that a major problem in U.S.-Panamanian relations was the lack of a central decision-making authority:

> Our ambassador in Panama has no control over Zone affairs and has too little influence on Zone-Panama relations. He can report his views and recommendations to the Secretary of State, who in turn can report to the President. The President may then call in the Secretary of the Army, who supervises the Governor of the Zone. While this circuitous process is under way, the Governor of the Zone is most likely talking with high Panamanian officials, including the President of the Republic. He is probably visiting with Panamanian businessmen. . . . In some respects, the governor, in his capacity as president of the Canal Company, feels he is more responsible to Congress—to which he must go each year for appropriations—than he is to the Secretary of the Army and the President.

This was the situation that had prevailed since the days of Colonel Goethals. Milton Eisenhower concluded that the U.S. government should speak with one voice, that of the ambassador.[29]

The single wage legislation of 1958 proved a slap in the face to Panamanians. Technically, U.S. and Panamanian citizens doing the same work would be paid equally, except the Americans would receive a 25 percent overseas bonus and longer vacations. As it was implemented, however, the U.S. work force continued to monopolize high-paying jobs (with the bonus, generous vacations, free schools and health care, and so on) and received a huge upgrade in salaries. Panamanians, on the other hand, stuck in low-paying jobs with limited benefits, received a minuscule upgrade and confronted further losses by the income tax provisions of the 1955 agreement.[30]

Panamanian students took the lead in expressing their anger over relations with the United States. In May 1958 they carried out "Operation Sovereignty," which included planting Panamanian flags in the Canal Zone and pressing the government for more schools and financial aid. The National Guard attacked the demonstrators, one of whom was killed. Students—who had long hated the police—responded with a huge funeral march that also erupted in street fighting. The government declared a state of siege and finally negotiated a truce with student leaders. A few months later the embassy recommended provision of nonlethal riot-control weapons to the guard, in anticipation of new demonstrations. This was the beginning of a new, violent phase in U.S.-Panamanian relations.[31]

Panama experienced new disorder and bloodshed in 1959, which in hindsight marked a major turning point in Panama's history. Inspired by Fidel Castro's successful toppling of an established government by guerrilla forces, Panamanian insurgents launched a revolt at Cerro Tute. In addition two invading forces landed, Cuban militiamen at Nombre de Dios and irregulars led by Harmodio Arias's son, Roberto, at Santa Clara. All three insurrections failed, but they heightened feelings of crisis.[32]

Domestic unrest began in October, when Colón labor leaders organized a "Hunger and Desperation March" to Panama City to demand higher wages, rent ceilings, land reform, low-cost housing, unemployment insurance, and price controls. The march disrupted traffic and services for several days and dramatized the distress experienced by the urban working class.[33]

The unrest spread to the Canal Zone on 3 November, the anniversary of independence. Led by prominent political figures, students entered the U.S. enclave to raise their flag and to assert Panama's sovereignty over it. As zone police and army units were called in, Panamanian sympathizers poured into the streets. American buildings were burned and scores of demonstrators were wounded. Order was only restored when the National Guard occupied the terminal cities. Less than a month later new riots broke out, which left eighteen casualties among zone defenders. The military summary concluded that these new riots "were better organized, involved larger crowds, and were more violent in their expression of anti-U.S. sentiments than were those of 3 November."[34]

For several years Eisenhower had been trying to "head off any developments . . . comparable to what had occurred in Egypt." The flag riots disturbed him, and he was apparently persuaded that their provenance lay not only in the failure to implement the 1955 treaty but also in the fundamental relationship set down in 1903. He sent a special emissary to assess the situation and to present Panama with a plan for improving relations between the two countries, which included an increase in Canal Zone procurement of goods in Panama to boost the economy and recognition of Panama's "titular sovereignty" over the zone. Eisenhower also concluded that a ceremonial display of Panama's flag in the zone would mollify the Panamanians.[35]

The Eisenhower administration also expanded foreign aid to Panama to alleviate unemployment and bolster the economy. In April 1960 the president announced a nine-point program to be carried out by a variety of agencies active in Panama—a 10 percent raise in wages for unskilled and semiskilled workers, training of Panamanians for higher-level positions, new local-rate housing, increased payments to retired canal workers, a boost in local-rate teachers' salaries, and a shift of jobs from U.S. to local-rate status. In addition the embassy agreed to arrange the construction of low-cost housing and a new water main to Panama City and to lower water fees. The entire package, which was called Operación Amistad (Operation Friendship), injected tens of millions of dollars into the Panamanian economy. Eisenhower appointed a new ambassador, Joseph Farland, to lead a new country team—comprised of the ambassador, a new Canal Zone governor, and a new commander-in-chief of the Caribbean Command—with explicit instructions to do all they could to eliminate irritations between the United States and Panama. Finally, in September the president ordered Panamanian flags to be flown alongside U.S. ones at the embassy and Shaler's Triangle in the zone.[36]

Behind the scenes, the 1958–59 riots produced a sea change in official U.S. thinking about Panama and the canal. It is best seen in the policy revisions of the National Security Council (NSC). On 30 January 1959, the NSC policy for Panama read: "Maintain in force all the rights, power, and authority granted the United States by the Convention of 1903 with Panama, as the basic treaty covering the status of the Canal Zone." The updated version of 16 February 1959, read: "No sound alternative has offered itself to the policy of maintaining U.S. rights under the Treaty of 1903, but interpretive problems and severe operational difficulties, including violence against the Zone, arose in the implementation of this policy in the light of the increasingly vola- tile situation prevailing in Panama."

By 15 November 1960, the NSC language had become more somber with regard to Latin America as a whole, due to the deterioration of relations with Cuba. Regarding Panama, the policy (which had been cleared with the president and the cabinet) read: "U.S. strategic and economic interests . . . will require the opening of a new sea-level canal across Central America by 1980 . . . and the United States will have to initiate and play a leading role in the financing of this project." The document went on to say that the United States should keep the old canal but try to reduce friction with Panama, shift control of binational affairs to the U.S. ambassador, and promote social and economic de- velopment in order to lessen Panama's dependence on the canal. The old canal could not be defended and would be obsolete within twenty years, and the zone was an insuperable obstacle to better relations with Panama. The solution was to build a sea-level canal, probably but not necessarily in Panama, and make a fresh start. Most likely nuclear excavation would be used, according to a study presented to the Panama Canal board of directors in early 1960.[37] Clearly, a new era of U.S.-Panamanian relations was at hand.

Eisenhower had made a last-ditch effort to improve U.S. relations with all Latin American nations in 1959 and 1960, partly in response to the Cuban Revolution and partly to aid Richard Nixon's presidential campaign. His boldest move was the creation of the Inter-American Development Bank (IDB), prompted by Brazilian President Juscelino Kubitschek's proposal of a huge development program for the hemi- sphere. The IDB, though undercapitalized, would soon serve as the centerpiece of the Alliance for Progress. Nevertheless, U.S. troubles with Panama, augmented by frustration with the 1955 treaty and by the flag riots, reverberated throughout the hemisphere. Panama should have been a showplace of U.S.-Latin cooperation and prosperity, but observers described the Panama Canal as "a body of water entirely surrounded by trouble." Eisenhower bought some breathing time with his concessions in 1959 and 1960, but in the long run the two countries would be forced to negotiate deeper changes in the way the Panama Canal operated. The old partnership had collapsed.

# 7 A Time of Troubles and Treaties, 1960–1979

On 9 January 1964, less than two months after the assassination of President John F. Kennedy, Panamanian students launched the largest assault on the Canal Zone in history. Ostensibly to force the display of Panama's flag, the action really expressed younger Panamanians' anger and frustration with their powerlessness in dealing with the colossus of the north. About two dozen Panamanians died and scores suffered gunshot wounds. For the first time in the U.S.-Panamanian alliance, the weak partner suspended diplomatic relations to dramatize the iniquity of the 1903 treaty, maintained in force by American soldiers.

## The Turbulent Decade

The decade of the 1960s proved pivotal in inter-American relations, a time of high U.S. involvement in Latin America and of dramatic changes in policy. The leftward plunge of the Castro government in Cuba, the U.S. Alliance for Progress, widespread guerrilla warfare, the Dominican invasion, and the rise of the so-called national security states in the southern cone dramatically altered relations among the countries of the hemisphere. The 1970s, in contrast, saw a retreat from U.S. involvement, to the posture Henry Kissinger dubbed "the low profile."[1]

Panama, too, became the focus of intense discussion and action during the 1960s, largely though not exclusively regarding the canal. Following new flag riots in 1964, the two countries negotiated a treaty package to replace the 1903 Hay–Bunau-Varilla convention. This failed to win ratification but later served as the basis for renewed nego-

tiations in the mid-1970s. These years of sporadic negotiations culminated in an intense debate over treaties signed in 1977 by U.S.
President Jimmy Carter and Panamanian strongman Omar Torrijos.
Not since the abortive Versailles Treaty had the U.S. Senate seen such
public involvement, both for and against the agreements. Finally, the
Senate approved them, but the effort weakened Carter politically and
helped pave the way to the White House for Ronald Reagan.

John F. Kennedy and Roberto Chiari won their respective 1960 presidential elections in the United States and Panama thanks largely to
their foreign policy platforms. Kennedy flayed the Eisenhower administration for "losing Cuba" and falling dangerously behind the USSR
in military preparedness. He promised to stem the growth of communism in Latin America and to reassert American leadership in the
region. Chiari pledged himself to overhaul relations with the United
States in order to end the old injustices and replace the despised 1903
treaty with a more modern one. He intended to shift national attention
from the canal, long the symbol of Yankee imperialism, to domestic programs of economic and social development. His slogan—"It's
time for a change"—signaled his desire for reform. To succeed he
would have to convince the nation's elites (to which he belonged) to
accept policies they had previously resisted. Yet hard as the two presidents tried, they failed to achieve an improvement in their countries'
relations.

In November 1960 the outgoing Eisenhower team pushed ahead
with implementation of the nine-point aid program, supplemented
with doses of cash to help the Chiari administration get on its feet. Five
million dollars constituted an emergency budget supplement, and
another million was earmarked for small social development projects
with high visibility. This was justified by the fact that a "successor
government might well be a Castro-oriented or inspired regime with
Communist leanings."[2] The cold war, heating up in the Caribbean
basin, definitely spurred the White House and State Department to
rethink Panama policies along the lines charted by the NSC.

Soon after taking office, Kennedy launched a huge new aid program, dubbed the Alliance for Progress, to pump $50 billion into Latin

American socioeconomic reform efforts. Panama (along with Brazil and Bolivia) was an early beneficiary of this initiative. The alliance undertook a wide range of programs to advance school construction, public utilities, housing, public health, community development, job training, roads, agrarian reform, and economic planning. In addition, scores of young Peace Corps volunteers fanned out through rural Panama to work in community improvement projects. United States Agency for International Development (USAID) expenditures in the early 1960s ran 600 percent over levels in the preceding decade. These programs, together with publicity issued by the U.S. Information Service, improved Panamanians' attitudes toward the United States but also whetted appetites for solutions to canal problems.[3]

In September 1961 Chiari sent a long letter to Kennedy requesting a thorough revision of the canal operations so that Panama would benefit more from its existence. Six weeks later Kennedy responded positively, saying he recognized that problems existed and would appoint a study group to resolve them. The interdepartmental committee he formed took the position that a total revision of the 1903 treaty would have to await plans for a sea-level canal, as determined by the NSC the year before. In the meantime, however, the government should do everything possible to help Panama economically and to improve relations with gestures of goodwill. The committee suggested some immediate palliatives, such as completion of the bridge over the canal, leasing canal docks in Colón to Panama, and an increase in aid disbursements. Some long-term recommendations required congressional approval, such as return of unneeded lands, transfer of jurisdiction over Panama's highway corridor through the zone, withholding income tax from canal workers' pay, and improvements in the employment structure.[4] Thus the chimerical sea-level canal delayed revision of the 1903 treaty yet also heightened Panamanian aspirations for massive new expenditures on construction.

Chiari was not satisfied with these promises, so Kennedy invited him to Washington in June 1962 for personal talks. The two presidents conferred on a range of issues during their two days together, thereby stepping up the level and breadth of negotiations, and appointed two representatives each to continue discussions. In mid-June Kennedy signed a secret memorandum to the effect that a new treaty would eventually be drafted, either to cover a sea-level canal or to revise the operations of the existing one. During the following year some progress was made toward correcting Chiari grievances. Two major steps in this direction were the inauguration of the bridge in October and the designation of fifteen Canal Zone sites where the two nations' flags would be flown side-by-side.[5]

Despite some progress, relations between the two countries remained rocky throughout 1963. Some problems were symbolic, others substantive. For example, Congress named the bridge after the Thatcher Ferry that it replaced, whereas Panamanians called it the Bridge of the Americas. (Panamanians and Americans clashed over the name on the day the bridge was opened.) A suit by a U.S. canal employee postponed the display of more flags in the zone. Congress failed to appropriate monies for the sea-level canal studies. And work on a long list of other requests by the Panamanians was stalled by protracted discussions with the Pentagon, the State Department, congressional committees, the Treasury Department, and others.[6] Chiari took sharp criticism from his countrymen for the lack of results.

Part of the problem was reluctance in many sectors of the U.S. government to make concessions to Panama. Some believed that any reforms would prompt the Panamanians to increase their demands. Congressman Daniel Flood called the decision to fly the Panamanian flag in the zone "another Munich," and Democrats in general opposed giving in to Panama. Governor Robert Fleming found administration of the Canal Zone in these years "one of the most frustrating experiences I ever had . . . because of the complexity of the interests involved. . . . every department of the United States government got into the act. . . . it took practically years for a simple, obvious problem to get recognized." For this reason the White House was often unable to enforce change in the Canal Zone and the Southern Command.[7]

When in August 1963 the popular Ambassador Joseph Farland resigned, U.S.-Panamanian relations took a nosedive because of doubts about the sincerity of U.S. intentions. The joint commission had finished its work the preceding month, and the Kennedy administration appeared unwilling to make any larger concessions or to budge on the sovereignty issue. Moreover, the U.S. approval of the Nuclear Test Ban Treaty in August 1963 appeared to rule out the possibility of nuclear excavation of a sea-level canal. Panamanians bitterly concluded that they had been deceived. The delay in selecting a successor to Farland heightened those beliefs. President Kennedy's assassination in November halted discussions regarding the Panama Canal, and President Lyndon B. Johnson rejected Kennedy's nominee for ambassador.[8] Relations between the two countries, therefore, drifted.

New flag riots erupted in January 1964.[9] They began on the seventh, when zone students disobeyed the governor's orders and raised the U.S. flag in front of Balboa High School. The act quickly became a symbol of zone residents' defiance Washington's concessions to Panama. Soon Panamanian students objected that this violated the recent practice of flying the two flags side-by-side. On the afternoon of the ninth, while the governor was away, scores of Panamanian students marched into the zone in order to raise their flag on the high school flagpole. This march led to a confrontation between the two groups, and in the scuffle the Panamanian flag was torn and some students injured. Word of the events spread quickly through Panama, and that evening thousands of people swarmed into the streets bordering the Canal Zone to express their rage at the United States. The canal police resisted attempts to invade the zone, using small arms and tear gas, while the Panamanian police stayed away. In view of the worsening situation, the commander-in-chief of the Southern Command took over the zone in what amounted to a state of siege. That evening the first Panamanian student was killed by a bullet. The next morning Chiari suspended relations with the United States, alleging unwarranted aggression against Panamanian demonstrators, and requested that the Rio Treaty of 1947 be invoked in order to investigate the conflict.

The rioting grew worse in the following days and ended only when the National Guard occupied the areas bordering the Canal Zone on the thirteenth. It had become a spectacular venting of hatred and anger by the Panamanians. The violence was random, disorganized, blind. Looting broke out in the cities when it became clear that the police would not intervene, and vandals set fire to buildings owned by U.S. corporations. When it was over, two dozen were dead and hundreds wounded. As William Jorden comments, the riots left a wound or trauma in the Panamanian psyche. Those who died were considered martyrs of the struggle against Yankee imperialism. Indeed, Panama changed the name of the street separating the capital and the zone, from Fourth of July Avenue to Avenue of the Martyrs.[10]

The riots were the first foreign crisis to confront Johnson, who had yet to appoint an ambassador to Panama. He sent emissaries to meet with Chiari the day after the fighting broke out and readily accepted an investigation by the Organization of American States. He believed that Chiari was attempting to use the riots to force U.S. concessions on the canal. Johnson responded by pressuring Chiari to control the rioting. After peace returned, the two presidents issued a joint promise to look into revising the 1903 treaty. Rejecting advice from the State Department hierarchy, Johnson chose economist Jack Vaughn for ambassador, and formal relations were restored by mid-year.[11]

### Negotiating the 1967 Treaties

Despite his early irritation with the Panamanians, Johnson gradually warmed to the idea of a new canal treaty, probably because respected associates persuaded him that the relationship needed to be modernized.[12] He also hoped that the process would be brief. In this spirit, exploratory talks went on during 1964, guided by two high-level bodies, the Panama Review Group in Washington, chaired by Thomas Mann, assistant secretary of state for inter-American affairs, and the Panama Review Committee, in Panama, headed by Ambassador Vaughn. Both made progress in defining the positions of the State Department and the Pentagon regarding minimum U.S. interests in Panama. State pushed for more Panamanian benefits from the canal, while the military insisted on preserving its bases there. The Pentagon was clearly the most influential player in these teams.[13]

Presidential elections in both countries delayed the start of serious negotiations for the remainder of 1964. Chiari passed on his mantle to his former interior minister, Marco Aurelio Robles in October, and the following month Johnson won a landslide victory in the United States. In the meantime, though, Congress had taken an important step in September by creating yet another group, the Interoceanic Study Committee, to examine the feasibility of a sea-level canal. It began work in April 1965 and published its report in 1970.

In a startling announcement in early December 1964, Johnson and his foreign policy team promised to abrogate the 1903 treaty. To do so required simultaneous negotiation of three new treaties: one dealing with operation of the lock canal for a set period of time; a second authorizing the United States to build a sea-level canal; and the last addressing the issue of military security and bases in the Canal Zone. Johnson announced this decision in a national television address. As a signal to the contentious Panamanians, however, he emphasized that the United States would approach other Central American countries about possible canal rights-of-way if talks with Panama stalled.[14]

Formal negotiations began in January 1965 for what came to be known as the three-in-one or 1967 treaties. The teams met in Washington, and the agenda flowed largely from what U.S. members decided to discuss. They had to clear myriad details with several government agencies while staying in touch with congressional committees.[15] By mid-1965 Johnson (supported by State) had acquiesced in a major Panamanian demand—zone management by a binational commission—and agreed to suspend talks about other Central American sea-level routes. And to sweeten the deal, the White House sped up disbursement of financial aid in Panama.

In September the two presidents announced agreement on several principles: abrogation of the 1903 treaty, U.S. recognition of Panama's effective sovereignty over the canal and integration of the zone into Panamanian national life, termination of the U.S. role in the lock canal upon a fixed date or when a sea-level canal began operations, fair wages and benefits for Panamanian employees, and a joint guarantee of the neutrality and defense of the waterway.

As the negotiators continued their work in 1966, the two presidents tried to line up support for the draft treaties. Johnson worked his charm on congressional leaders and bullied the Pentagon. As his aide Walt Rostow wrote, "We . . . need[ed] a good negotiation plus a good development program plus first-rate political and psychological leadership in Panama and at home to turn this corner in history."[16] Robles faced greater obstacles. Riots in Colón in June and a cabinet crisis in Panama City stalled talks. He began to worry that maneuvering for the May 1968 presidential election could stir up opposition to the agreements. The U.S. government appropriated $3 million for a community development program to calm public discontent in Panama's terminal city slums, but the sheer complexity of the treaties worked against both presidents because the longer talks dragged on the more distrustful the public became.[17]

Anxiety rose during the early months of 1967, as the negotiators raced the clock. Robles urged Johnson to hurry the talks so that he could present treaties to his National Assembly by mid-year. They managed to initial drafts by June, and the two countries proudly announced that the treaties would be signed shortly.

The draft treaties were leaked to the press before either president could brief his respective legislative leaders, so a great deal of public debate erupted in July. The treaties were complicated and far-reaching, and the effect of the leak was to give virtually everybody something to criticize. Thus time and public opinion both turned against their ratification.

The 1967 treaties were remarkable in many respects. By abrogating the Hay–Bunau-Varilla convention, they eliminated one of the most visible symbols of early twentieth-century U.S. imperialism. Yet this was done peacefully through negotiation. They also set up a binational commission to manage the waterway, effectively granting Panama a say in its operation. The chief administrator would be a U.S. citizen and his deputy a Panamanian, both appointed by the U.S. president. The board would be composed of five Americans and four Panamanians. Most of the lands in the former Canal Zone would be returned to Panama, and the streamlined Canal Area that replaced it would have a government limited to basic services. Panama would derive new revenues from the canal, in a profit-sharing arrangement. The treaty would expire on 31 December 1999, or a year after completion of a sea-level canal, whichever came first. The only precedent for a binational international utility like this was the Saint Lawrence Seaway administered by the United States and Canada.

The second and third treaties covered defense and sea-level plans. One pledged the two countries to protect the canal and guarantee its neutrality, and it regularized existing military bases with a Status of Forces Agreement (SOFA) running into the next century. The other authorized the United States to build, singly or in consortium with other countries, a sea-level canal, which would be operated jointly, in the same way as the lock waterway.

By the time the treaties were ready they had to be shelved. Opinion among leading politicians in Panama ran against approval, and the Assembly actually impeached Robles in mid-1967 for his role in the negotiations. He stayed in office only by virtue of the support of the guard. He had no hope of getting the treaties approved. Johnson also tabled the treaties since he did not want to send them to the Senate without prior ratification by Panama. Besides, he already had his hands full conducting the Vietnam War and defending it at home. When the treaties were set aside, the aid program designed to facilitate their acceptance was curtailed.

Robles's crisis in 1967 was not entirely due to adverse reception of the treaty drafts. He had also made powerful enemies among Panama's elites by pushing for economic reforms. His minister of finance, David Samudio, had sponsored a new law that, if enforced, would have taxed two major industries (sugar and cement) for the first time, raised taxes on land, and boosted contributions from wealthy citizens in general. This drove many politicians out of Robles's camp, especially when it became known that he supported the unpopular Samudio as his successor in the 1968 presidential elections. So the country seemingly rejected a new treaty and Robles himself.

Arnulfo Arias proved to be the beneficiary of Robles's misfortune. One after another government politician switched to Arias's Panameñista party, so that the opposition candidate experienced a tidal wave of support. As Arias's popularity grew, the top commander of the National Guard decided to withdraw the service's traditional objection to Arias and to allow free elections. With regard to the United States, Arias's stance had moderated over the years. Although he voiced criticism of the 1967 treaties, he would probably have approved some version of the arrangements if he could receive credit for negotiating them. The U.S. embassy expressed no objections to Arias's candidacy and remained neutral in the May 1968 elections, which he won handily.[18]

### The 1968 Coup

Arias took the presidential oath on 1 October 1968, for the third time in his long and checkered career. He had formed an unbeatable coalition for the election. In addition, he had neutralized the guard with a sweetheart deal for the commander-in-chief, Bolívar Vallarino, and assurances that he would not disrupt the existing command structure. Once Vallarino was taken care of, however, Arias planned to replace key officers known to be opposed to the new president. Two of these were Major Boris Martínez and Colonel Omar Torrijos, senior officers with considerable time in rank. Martínez and a dozen others had formed the conspiratorial "Combo" in preceding months to prevent an Arias raid on their ranks and perhaps to carry out a preventive coup. But given assurances of guard integrity, they did not act before Arias's inauguration.

In the early days of his presidency, however, Arias revealed his intention to replace top guard officials with persons in whom he confided. So Martínez and the other members of Combo went ahead with their plans for a coup. They carried it out on the night of 11 October with virtually no bloodshed.[19] The U.S. ambassador, unaware of its execution, was away from his post. Two middle-echelon guard officers were named to a temporary junta, but Martínez was the undoubted power behind the scenes. The U.S. government, caught by surprise, responded coolly and even suspended relations for a month.

The plotters sought to forestall transfers and retirements of certain guard officers, so they had little in the way of a program and initially said nothing of the treaties signed with the United States the previous year. When efforts to form a civilian government failed, the real power increasingly concentrated in the clique of officers who surrounded Martínez. Among them was Omar Torrijos. Arias, meanwhile, had fled into the zone and remained there for about ten days as a political exile. This heightened the impression that the U.S. government continued to support Arias and to oppose the junta. In fact U.S. officials had no coherent position regarding the coup, save for a preference for a government that would not threaten the canal. When the Nixon administration took over, Panama received even less attention from Washington.

The junta did issue a program in early 1969. Its inspiration lay in the pseudopopulist military regime of General Juan Velasco Alvarado in Peru and in the Civic Action training most officers had received in the Canal Zone. Invoking the precedent of the Alliance for Progress, the junta's program called for economic growth and social justice, good government, more foreign investment, and anticommunism. It sought to calm foreign fears of radicalism while offering reforms to the downtrodden at home. It accomplished neither goal.[20]

In February 1969, Torrijos shouldered out Martínez because of a conflict in programs, personalities, and styles.[21] Torrijos had built a strong following among senior and junior officers, which he used to consolidate power. He then attempted to build a coalition of civilian forces that would bolster his authority, but the effort proved elusive. Labor unions, students, intellectuals, business groups, political parties, and the U.S. government all remained distant or in opposition to the regime.

In December 1969, while Torrijos and several colleagues were traveling in Mexico, three guard officers seized power in Panama and declared Torrijos deposed. Their main reasons were growing communist influence within the government and Torrijos's dictatorial rule. Encouragement for the coup came from politicians and the business community, though the details remain murky. Torrijos returned to David, where an officer loyal to him, Manuel Antonio Noriega, commanded a garrison with about 20 percent of the total guard troops. Together they began an overland march toward the capital, gathering military and civilian supporters along the way. Within a day after arriving in the capital they arrested the coup leaders and restored Torrijos to power.[22]

Frustrated by the civilian resistance to him, Torrijos then veered to the left in an attempt to capture a broad base of support from workers. His new labor minister, Rómulo Bethancourt, unveiled a plan for government-sponsored obligatory unionization that would boost workers' leverage with owners.[23] Meanwhile, Torrijos took to the road to spread his promise of better wages and working conditions. He wore fatigues and toured the countryside by jeep, much the way Castro had in the early 1960s. Eventually he would promulgate a progressive labor code that earned him some support. He was gradually transforming himself into a reformist military ruler, a rare phenomenon in Latin America.[24]

In its profession and conduct, the Torrijos regime appeared variously as revolutionary, reformist, populist, dictatorial, and socialist, but in the final analysis it was none of these. Its ambiguous, shifting nature certainly affected Panama's relationship with the United States, but the legacy of the regime has yet to be fully understood.[25] Basically, Torrijos was an inspired improviser with a great capacity for booze and small talk and little stomach for day-to-day administration. He was willing to shake up the country and its government, step on elite toes, bluff the gringos, and above all spend money freely. He was an old-fashioned nationalist who wanted Panama to have a bigger piece of the canal pie, but he was also a willful leader who sometimes used force and even murder to intimidate opponents and to stay in power. He and his staff proved expert in manipulating nationalist symbols, so that by the end of the 1970s Torrijos enjoyed a charisma achieved by only one other Panamanian leader, Arnulfo Arias. In the end, Torrijos won support in most sectors of Panamanian society and so was beholden to none, save the guard itself.

Ironically, these very qualities helped produce the dramatic changes in U.S.-Panamanian relations symbolized by the 1977 treaties. Torrijos's insistence on abrogating the 1903 treaty brought real pressure to bear in Washington, and his dictatorial rule meant that the pressure would not abate quickly. Finally, his domination of the National Guard kept him in power long enough to finish negotiating new treaties. It is very unlikely that the treaties could have been concluded without him.[26]

Working with Torrijos required fancy footwork by the United States. His vanity and machismo had to be fed, his spending spree financed, his forays into international organizations parried, and his constantly shifting image filtered for U.S. consumption. In the early 1970s these tasks were simple enough, but by mid decade they had become a full-scale campaign of damage control.[27] While Torrijos remained the driving force in the background, his negotiating team changed over time. Several black intellectuals from the University of Panama played important roles in the talks. The fact that many high guard officers were of mixed race prompted comments that advocates of the treaties were nonwhite leaders representing the disenfranchised masses, despite evidence that the overwhelming majority of Panamanians—whatever their race, ethnic background, social class, or ideology—wished to abrogate the 1903 treaty and replace it with a fairer one. The minority that opposed the new treaty did so for a variety of reasons, but it did not represent any social or racial group. In short, the 1970s treaty talks cannot be explained by a simple class-interest model.

## Treaty-Making with Torrijos

Throughout 1970 and 1971, Torrijos consolidated his power and developed a leftist-nationalist program, while the U.S. government paid little attention to Panama. Torrijos made contact with Fidel Castro, who a few years later would become a friend. He rejected U.S. demands for a long-term renewal of the Rio Hato army base, which reverted to Panamanian control. American officials privately tried to induce Torrijos to moderate his stance by emulating the Brazilian military, but they did not succeed. Symptomatic of the cool relations with the United States was a formal rejection of the 1967 treaties by the foreign ministry in the fall of 1970.

Nevertheless, the State Department, fearing renewed riots if relations deteriorated further, urged President Nixon to revive canal talks in 1971. During a chance visit with Torrijos's civilian president, Demetrio "Jimmy" Lakas, Nixon proposed such talks, and Lakas accepted. Teams were assembled and discussions took place in Washington. José Antonio de la Ossa, Fernando Manfredo, and Carlos López Guevara made up the Panamanian side, with the later participation of Diógenes de la Rosa. Robert Anderson, who had presided over the 1965–67 treaty talks as well as the sea-level canal study, chaired the U.S. team. Unlike earlier negotiations, however, these did not have the full support or even interest of the respective heads of state. The U.S. team pulled back from concessions made earlier, while the Panamanians pushed to go beyond the 1967 drafts. Negotiations stalled by mid-1972, and Torrijos ended them in December.[28]

The Panamanian leadership was not inactive during 1972, however. Torrijos had convoked a constitutional assembly, which obediently approved a charter drafted by the administration, named Torrijos chief of state, and afforded him a degree of legitimacy. Cleverly he pressed the issue of sovereignty by designating polling places in the Canal Zone, which he called Panama's "tenth province." He also encouraged expansion of the international banking industry, which according to the 1970 law could maintain accounts and process transactions in secrecy.[29] Finally, Torrijos actively pursued socioeconomic policies associated with the UN Economic Commission on Latin America and the Alliance for Progress: import substitution industrialization, a pro-union labor code, agrarian reform, redistribution of income, housing, public health, education, and rural development in general. Such dramatic moves earned him the sobriquet, Torrijos the populist. Cynics, however, termed him a false populist because he lacked genuine commitment to the poor.[30]

Behind the scenes, Panama pursued a new strategy for forcing the United States to make concessions regarding the canal. Foreign Minister Juan Antonio Tack and UN Ambassador Aquilino Boyd focused their efforts on the UN Security Council, where Panama occupied a temporary seat. Boyd worked assiduously, with the help of Torrijos and Tack, to persuade UN delegates and friendly heads of state that Panama's position was just. They hoped to bring the weight of world public opinion to bear on the United States in order to force the colossus into more serious negotiations. Specifically, Tack hoped to move the venue to Panama, where proceedings would be open to public view and he could mobilize international opinion against the United States.[31]

The Panamanians succeeded in convincing a majority of the Security Council members to vote in favor of a meeting in Panama in March 1973. The United States had tried but failed to prevent this move, so it fell to Henry Kissinger, national security adviser, to help contain the damage Tack planned for the United States. As expected, Torrijos addressed the council with a passionate call to overhaul the relationship between his country and the United States. Meanwhile, friendly diplomats circulated several draft resolutions dealing with the canal. In the coming days efforts were made to produce a compromise that the United States could accept. In the end, however, Torrijos and his team decided to hold out for a version they knew the United States would veto, in order to draw greater attention to their cause. The final vote was thirteen yeas, one nay (the United States), and one abstention (Great Britain). This was only the third time in history the United States had exercised its veto power, a fact that helped generate publicity for the session. At the end of the meeting, Tack announced, "The United States has vetoed Panama, but the world has vetoed the United States!"[32] Kissinger later acknowledged that the Panamanians had scored a victory with their tactics. Within two months a NSC-drafted report by President Nixon to Congress stated that the time had come to establish a new relationship with Panama.

Sensing the weakening U.S. resolve, Tack proposed a set of broad principles to energize the stalled negotiations. These stipulated that the 1903 treaty would be replaced by one with a fixed termination date and formal recognition of Panama's sovereignty and jurisdiction over the zone and its works. In return for an equitable share of the profits,

Panama would grant to the United States the power to manage and protect the canal. The two countries would also agree on conditions under which the lock canal could be replaced by a sea-level canal.

The negotiations accomplished little during the remainder of 1973. Kissinger shifted from the NSC to State, and Ellsworth Bunker, former ambassador to South Vietnam, became U.S. negotiator for Panama Canal talks. Under Bunker's skillful management, talks proceeded into 1974, when Kissinger flew to Panama and signed a version of the Tack principles. The main differences in the final document were provisions for joint management and defense and the possibility of building an expanded (but not necessarily sea-level) canal.[33]

Already a potent opposition movement to block any alterations to the 1903 treaty had formed in the United States. Led initially by outspoken members of Congress, among them representatives Daniel Flood and John Murphy and senators Jesse Helms and Strom Thurmond, the opposition soon recruited California Governor Ronald Reagan, who used the Panama Canal treaty talks to gain national attention. Across the country, meanwhile, individuals and groups began mobilizing against treaty talks, and they soon constituted a grass-roots lobby with formidable resources—retired military officers, former canal employees and their relatives, academics, and the prov-erbial little old ladies in tennis shoes. When the treaties reached the Senate in 1978, the opposition resembled a patriotic, and often jingo-istic, crusade.[34]

Early on, however, the administration was more concerned with potential enemies of the treaties within the government. When nego-tiations began in earnest in mid-1974, the Bunker team made a special effort to win early support from the Pentagon. An informal working group brought together State and Pentagon officials to deal with the complexities of writing a new canal treaty. They began with the joint administration principle that had been part of the 1967 drafts, then moved on to canal neutrality, guaranteed by the United States and Panama and endorsed by means of a multilateral protocol. At this point talks slowed because of the succession from Nixon to Gerald Ford in August and because of a dispute over banana taxes.[35]

The slowdown prompted Torrijos to raise the stakes by reestablish-

ing diplomatic relations with Cuba. This created the specter of communist influence in Panama. Torrijos had had dealings with Fidel Castro
since 1971, when he helped negotiate the release of a Panamanian-
flag vessel being held by the Cubans. Now, it seemed, the implied
threat of a permanent relationship with Cuba might induce the United
States to bargain more seriously.[36]

The next item on the agenda, at the insistence of the Pentagon, was
a Status of Forces Agreement (SOFA) to authorize continued operation of military bases in Panama. Under the authority of the 1903
treaty regarding protection and defense of the canal, the U.S. military
had built fourteen bases in the Canal Zone. Panamanians had long
argued that these bases, which contained sophisticated matériel and
over ten thousand troops went far beyond local defense and in fact
served U.S. strategic purposes in Latin America. On those grounds,
Panama wanted a SOFA modeled on those for other U.S. overseas
bases. The Pentagon adopted the position that the canal treaty could
be revised but that U.S. strategic interests (that is, the bases) be guaranteed as a sine qua non. The negotiating teams pushed ahead and
drafted a SOFA that consolidated the fourteen bases into four. It was
initialed in February 1975.[37]

Other items were discussed during the winter of 1974 and spring of
1975, such as the annuity Panama would receive and the lands and
waters that would be returned immediately to Panama. The United
States also dropped its request for authorization to build a sea-level
canal, the technical parameters of which were no longer attractive.
But the cycles of talks slowed again in mid-1975, as opposition grew
in Congress and elsewhere. Pentagon officials became so demanding that Bunker scarcely made any progress with the Panamanians.
Finally, in September, two understandings were reached: the Pentagon reluctantly gave its approval to a new treaty but insisted that
signing the final document follow the U.S. presidential elections in
November 1976.[38]

Throughout 1976 Bunker's team made very little progress on writing a new treaty. Aquilino Boyd replaced Tack as Panamanian chief
negotiator. Indeed, Ronald Reagan's campaign in the Republican pri-

mary elections generated considerable opposition to any change. The sole optimistic sign in the fall campaign was Democratic candidate Jimmy Carter's statement that relations with Panama ought to be reviewed with an eye toward increasing Panama's role in and profits from canal operations. His comment did little to soothe Torrijos, who became edgy and impatient. Random bomb explosions in the Canal Zone raised fears that Torrijos might resort to violent action to pressure or punish the United States. In December CIA director George Bush met with Panama's Foreign Minister Boyd and Noriega (chief of intelligence) to try to calm the situation before it led to a complete suspension of negotiations.

When Carter took office in January 1977, he called for a full review of the treaty situation, and soon the White House was committed to starting up negotiations again, using the Tack-Kissinger principles. Meanwhile, the secretary of state recruited corporate lawyer and diplomatic troubleshooter Sol Linowitz to assist Bunker in negotiations. One Panamanian negotiator described Linowitz as a catalyst, and another as a tough and energetic force to complement Bunker's nice-guy approach.[39]

The 1977 talks got off to a rocky start, with further changes in the teams and testing of positions. Finally, however, in May the last major obstacle to the treaties—acceptance by Panama of the U.S. right to guarantee the neutrality of the canal beyond the termination date of the canal treaty—was overcome. In exchange for this "bitter pill" the Panamanians received liberal concessions of lands and waters. With this obstacle removed, negotiations proceeded toward a final draft.[40]

Throughout the summer the negotiators worked away at the main treaty covering canal operations. The two country ambassadors, Gabriel Lewis and William Jorden, who had been instrumental in achieving agreement on the neutrality treaty, served as a shadow team to keep up communication and progress. At several points the process slowed because the Panamanians pushed for a large lump-sum payment and more annuities than the U.S. side believed it could sell to Congress. In the end, the Panamanians accepted most of the financial arrangements proposed by the Americans.[41] The basic outline of the treaty package, finished by mid-July, closely resembled that of 1967, though a great deal of drafting and vetting lay ahead. Negotiators then moved to Panama City in August for the final round of talks. There the Panamanian delegation again introduced a new element—its own draft developed independently of the one written in Washington— but the U.S. team rejected its counterparts' draft and the negotiators concluded their labor several days later.[42]

Now that the heads of state had agreed on the final elements of the treaties, lawyers and diplomats rushed to compose the final package—too hurriedly, as events turned out. The treaties were signed on 7 September 1977 in a Washington ceremony attended by most Latin American heads of state. It was a moment of great exultation for those who favored new treaties with Panama but a call to arms for those who opposed the changes. Linowitz wrote: "We all recognized that we had done only the first half of the job. What we did not understand yet was that this first half had been less arduous, less complicated, and less emotional than the task that lay ahead."[43]

## Ratification of the 1977 Treaties

Even before the treaties were finished, President Carter, Linowitz, and other figures prominent in the negotiations (especially from the Pentagon) began an intense campaign to win over public opinion and the Senate for the ratification. They approached newspaper editors, state governors, politically active citizens, businessmen, and opinion makers in general. They met almost daily with congressional leaders. In opposition, however, were arrayed perhaps one hundred thousand citizens who constituted an informal Panama Canal lobby to defeat ratification. The opposition outdid the supporters in mobilizing volunteer labor and raising cash. The debate raged across the country, energizing the citizenry and the media as few other foreign policy issues had. In the end, the proponents lost the public opinion battle, because it was easier to convince people to retain the status quo than to persuade them of the intangible benefits of complicated new legal and defense arrangements in Central America. It was soon clear that Americans still ached from defeat in Vietnam and could not countenance yielding a bastion so close to the American sense of destiny. Polls showed public opinion running steadily against the treaties.

One of the high points in the public deliberations was a debate between conservatives William F. Buckley, editor of the *National Review*, and Ronald Reagan. The first argued that "the United States, by signing these treaties, is better off militarily, is better off economically, and is better off spiritually." Reagan, who strongly criticized the administration for allegedly paying Panama to accept America's birthright, argued that "the world would see it as . . . a case where Uncle Sam put his tail between his legs and crept away rather than face trouble." In the end, the American public tended to see this issue as Reagan did— as a matter of national pride and rights.[44] An oft-cited observation on the canal was a remark by semanticist-turned-senator S. I. Hayakawa, "We stole it fair and square."[45]

In mid-October, as the Senate deliberated, Carter and Torrijos met in Washington to clarify controversial aspects of the Neutrality Treaty. Panama wanted assurances that the treaty would not permit U.S. intervention in domestic affairs, whereas the Senate insisted that the United States have the right to defend the canal unilaterally and to transit its warships ahead of all other vessels. The two presidents issued a "Statement of Understanding" along these lines, hoping to mollify critics in both countries. These provisions were eventually incorporated into the treaty as a full amendment.

Carter had made clear that the U.S. Senate would not consent to the treaties without Panama's prior acceptance, so Torrijos conducted a plebiscite on 23 October that gave him a two-thirds majority. The Statement of Understanding, apparently, persuaded Panamanians that the days of unilateral intervention would be ended under the new treaties. Still, some important intellectual and political leaders (many in exile) opposed the treaties.

Meanwhile the Senate had begun its hearings on the two treaties that constituted the proposed Panama Canal arrangements. Bunker and Linowitz had purposely separated the neutrality from the management issues in hope that senators who were confident that the canal would remain under the U.S. defense umbrella would more readily approve the changed operating agreement. Soon, however, ambiguity in the neutrality treaty raised problems for its advocates: Panamanian leaders held that the treaty did *not* authorize unilateral U.S. intervention to protect the canal, whereas U.S. spokesmen had assured Congress that it did. The junior senator from Arizona, Dennis DeConcini, managed to tack on a proviso to the first treaty in order to plug the security "loophole": his reservation gave the United States an unrestricted right to intervene in Panama in order to protect the canal. Panamanians objected that this was a throwback to the days of gunboat diplomacy, but the reservation went through and the treaty passed in March 1978, by a vote of 68 to 32.[46]

During the next month the Senate worked on the operations treaty. The bipartisan leadership managed to counteract the effects of the DeConcini reservation by adding to the main treaty language assuring that nothing in the treaties would "have as its purpose or be interpreted as a right of intervention in the internal affairs of the Republic of Panama." This amendment, sponsored by Senators Robert Byrd and Howard Baker, echoed the terms of the previous Statement of Understanding and pleased Panamanians.

As the debate progressed, it became clear that the senators considered many different factors before making up their minds: public opinion, favors from the White House, their reelection plans, the correctness of the treaties themselves, and the possible repercussions of rejecting them. The vote came on 18 April, with the same count: 68 to 32. It climaxed thirteen years of discussions and negotiations, and the emotionally charged climate of the day recalled that long struggle.

Treaty ratification caused great joy in Panama and among U.S. supporters. The only bittersweet note was Torrijos's revelation that had the Senate rejected the treaty, his troops would have invaded and attacked the canal the next day. The decision made on 18 April stands high on the list of momentous foreign policy choices taken in the United States in this century. The only other treaty ratification battle that compares with the canal debates was that over joining the League of Nations—which was rejected. David McCullough pronounced the vote a "watershed," perhaps equal to the construction of the canal itself. Supporters and opponents, of course, had differing interpretations of the vote: the former regarded it as a historic act of statesmanship and a reaffirmation of American respect for the sovereignty of all nations large and small; the latter saw it as a giveaway and surrender that weakened U.S. security and diminished its world standing. Both sides agreed, however, on the gravity of the choice.

Regardless of the differing evaluations of the treaties, things began to improve in Panama almost immediately. There was a euphoric image of the future. Torrijos, now in his tenth year as dictator, pulled back from active governance of the country—"returned to the barracks," he said, in favor of his hand-picked president, Aristides Royo —to resume his command of the National Guard and bask in the glory of his accomplishment. An OAS commission examining human rights in Panama nudged Torrijos in the direction of a civilian-run democracy. Most Panamanians waited optimistically for the implementation of the treaties, scheduled for 1 October 1979. A few groups, to be sure, stood to lose in the transition. The Zonians, who had been preparing for the worst for some time, continued to leave in large numbers as new U.S. personnel rotated in to take their places.[47] The West Indian descendants who still lived in the Canal Zone also suffered hardships, for their residences and most of their jobs would soon come under Panama's jurisdiction. This was especially true of employees of the Panama Railroad and the port facilities.

The U.S. House of Representatives reserved an unpleasant surprise for the White House and Panama, however, for that body had to initiate legislation to implement many parts of the canal treaty. Representatives, who had to face their constituents every two years, felt a great deal of pressure against the treaties, yet they were denied any role in the ratification process. The administration, to make its job easier, claimed that the House had no role to play until after the treaties were ratified. Many representatives believed otherwise, because the treaty mandated disposal of government property. The House did not take up legislation on the canal until after the November 1978 elections, and then several treaty opponents wrote their own versions designed to hamstring treaty implementation or punish the White House. When the administration submitted its draft bill in January 1979 and asked for action by the end of May, a number of representatives revolted. They shelved the administration version and fell in behind a draft prepared by New York Democrat John Murphy, a longtime treaty foe.[48]

The House took its time deliberating on the Panama Canal arrangements and did what it could to counteract the administration's plans. Treaty framers had envisioned a canal run by a semiautonomous, binational commission of five U.S. and four Panamanian members to set general policy and approve budgets and procedures in a manner befitting an independent government corporation. The bill that finally passed in September (called the Panama Canal Act or Murphy Law after its sponsor) made the commission a dependency of the Department of Defense and required it to seek yearly approval from Congress for its budget and activities. A number of other measures, some in violation of the treaty, moved Ambassador Jorden to call the law "something between a misfortune and a disaster." It was the House's way of venting its anger at Carter and Panama.[49]

Conservative leaders in Congress—including Murphy, Jesse Helms, and Charles Wilson—also dragged their feet on the Panama Canal legislation in order to force the Carter administration to give fuller backing to the dictator of Nicaragua, Anastasio Somoza, who was in imminent danger of being defeated by the Sandinista revolutionaries. Their main strategy was to hold the legislation hostage, though they justified it on the grounds that Torrijos was helping the Sandinistas with arms and volunteers. Somoza's fall in July ended that tactic.

The House and Senate eventually reconciled their differences over the implementing legislation, and they approved it in late September, five days before the 1 October deadline. The treaties entered into effect, and the odyssey was over. The principals in the negotiations mostly dispersed. A few wrote books and memoirs about the experience; it had been an emotional, unforgettable process.

The two decades that elapsed between the flag riots of 1959 and the Panama Canal Act of 1979 saw a thorough change in the relations between the United States and Panama. Those who favored revising the

1903 treaty and who predicted an early conclusion could not have been more wrong. The task had been made far more difficult by concurrent developments within the two countries themselves. The United States—a benevolent but undisputed world power in 1960—had by 1979 lost a war in Vietnam and seen its government disgraced by malfeasance in the White House and elsewhere. Americans now wanted to "stand tall" again and to demand respect abroad. The election of Ronald Reagan in 1980 was the culmination of that shift in U.S. public sentiment. By the same token, Panama—a weak, dependent client state in 1960—had undergone a process of nation-building, albeit at the hands of military leaders and others hostile to the traditional elites. By 1979 Panamanians had become more unified and committed to becoming a genuine nation-state. So the apparently easy task of replacing an outmoded treaty with a modern one turned into a historic process, for each country was working out its own new identity at the same time that it tried to deal with the other's.

The 1977 Panama Canal treaties represent not just a turning point in U.S.-Panamanian relations but also a dividing line in U.S. policies toward all Third World countries. The ideal of a new international order born in the United Nations Charter in 1945 had been embodied in the 1977 treaties, yet the U.S. House of Representatives and voters in 1980 apparently disavowed them. During the next decade the world seemed to return to older ways: those of big powers and weak states, spheres of influence, covert intelligence operations, coercive diplomacy, and outright invasions. Yet neither the United States nor the Soviet Union had the resolve to impose a lasting imperial order on the world. Instead, great power policies in the 1980s probed, experimented, withdrew, and drifted. U.S.-Panamanian relations in the 1980s exemplified this aimlessness.

# 8    Treaty Implementation, 1979–1985

A light plane cut through the tropical rain in August 1981, carrying Panamanian strongman Omar Torrijos and a few companions over dense jungles in the central part of the country. Suddenly it plunged into the trees and exploded, killing all those aboard. Searchers took several days to find the wreckage, and mystery yet surrounds the cause of the crash. [Panamanians mourned the loss of Torrijos, who for better or worse had ruled for a dozen years and had signed new canal treaties with the United States.] Others would have to oversee their implementation.

Most persons who supported the new canal treaties expected that Panama would enjoy an unprecedented boom once they were implemented and that relations between the two countries would become amicable. More top-level jobs would go to Panamanians; the railroad, ports, and 58 percent of the old Canal Zone would fall under their jurisdiction; much new business would be shifted to Panama; and transfers of funds would run far above what they had in the past. While these expectations largely came true, their realization has not brought peace and prosperity to Panama nor friendly relations with the United States. Panama's economy wallowed in debt and stagnation for most of the 1980s. [The death of Torrijos left a political vacuum that was later filled by former intelligence chief Manuel Antonio Noriega.] Relations with the United States in the 1980s—which centered on treaty implementation, Central American affairs, the drug trade, and finally democratization—were uncertain and occasionally stormy. Treaty implementation has been the only area of success. Other issues generated much acrimony and conflict.

## Treaty Enactment

Though controversial, the 1979 Panama Canal Act required prompt implementation. President Carter chose the former commander of Southern Command, Lieutenant General Denis "Phil" McAuliffe, to be administrator of the Panama Canal. McAuliffe had served for over four years in Panama and, though not directly involved in the negotiations, was intimately familiar with them. He had supported the treaties and was willing to dedicate the remainder of his career to making them work. Torrijos nominated Fernando Manfredo to be deputy administrator. Manfredo had taken part in treaty talks since the early 1970s and was considered one of the least judgmental and constructive members of the Panamanian team. Moreover, he had avoided making enemies in Panama, an important quality for his effectiveness there. These choices—praised by knowledgeable observers at the time—proved to be correct, and to them must go much of the credit for the successful implementation of the treaties.[1]

Under McAuliffe's leadership, the canal administration had two priorities: to move ships through the canal quickly and safely and to train Panamanians to take over skilled and managerial jobs. This was done without alienating the Zonians, most of whom decided to stay on and see how matters worked out under the treaty. McAuliffe's scrupulous respect for the treaty and Panama Canal Act made them into the "law of the land," above question and challenge. For the first several years of the new regime, shipping through the canal increased, reaching an all-time record in 1982 due in part to passage of tankers carrying Alaskan North Slope oil. A 9.8 percent toll boost in 1983 raised income as well. Then traffic dropped sharply due to the world recession and the opening of a pipeline through western Panama, which took about half of the Alaskan oil destined for the East Coast. Since the mid-1980s transits through the canal have remained fairly stable but tonnage and tolls have risen because of an increase in the capacity of wide-beam and PANAMAX vessels and shipments of Japanese automobiles to the East Coast.[2] Little new growth was expected through the early 1990s, however.

The success in maintaining shipping traffic was complemented by a program to recruit and place more Panamanians in skilled, technical, and managerial jobs. Several million dollars a year were dedicated to apprenticeship and training programs, especially in the industrial trades. By 1990, it was estimated, canal personnel were 88 percent Panamanian, and one official projected an increase to 95 percent by 1999. The attrition rate among U.S. personnel ran about 100 to 150 per year, mostly due to retirements. Qualified Panamanians moved up the management ladder to head departments and divisions, a process expected to continue in the 1990s. The job security of Panamanians, however, was much on the minds of canal administrators, who noted that Panama's lack of civil service protection worried some employees, who feared they would lose their jobs in the canal turnover in 1999. By the same token, more U.S. employees (especially those eligible for early retirement) might leave after the Panamanian administrator took over in January 1990.

Several personnel issues had to be resolved in addition to raising the percentage of Panamanian employees. First, the administration instituted collective bargaining under the terms of legislation current in the United States, and by 1986 virtually every employee was covered by a union contract. Panama at first opposed this move but then allowed it on the grounds that it raised salaries. Second, the mid-1970s pay scale, the Panama Area Wage Base, originally accepted by Panama as a means to keep canal salaries in line with national rates, came under attack as discriminatory against Panamanians. Government negotiators had anticipated a large cash transfer from the United States. When this did not materialize, they adopted the strategy of maximizing wages and benefits their nationals would earn and spend in the local economy. Between 1983 and 1985, then, the canal converted to the Panama Canal Employment System, a single schedule that closely resembled the old merit system of the 1960s. The annual payroll cost of the conversion was about $3 million, and the cumulative total will be about $300 million by 1999. The new system simplified management by equalizing Panamanian and U.S. employee wages, and it also aided in recruitment and retention. Third, canal administrators convinced the Department of Defense to adopt the new wage system on military bases in Panama in order to create a uniform labor market. The orderliness of this personnel transition gratified senior canal officials and contributed to the success of treaty implementation.

Several thousand canal workers lost their jobs in the transition, however, because their activities were eliminated or transferred to Panama. Personnel authorities created elaborate rules for reductions in force, whereby persons whose jobs were eliminated could move down the ladder in order to stay on the payroll. Those actually let go were given preference in rehiring, and within two years officials believed that they had accommodated all those wishing to return to canal employment.

The Panama Canal Act had also established a special immigration category for non–U.S. citizen canal employees who lost their jobs or simply wished to leave Panama: fifteen thousand such persons were qualified for admission to the United States over and above existing national-origin quotas. In the end, less than two thousand visas were issued under this program, which suggested that workers adapted successfully to the new treaty and legislation.[3]

Other aspects of the transition occurred smoothly also. In April 1982 Panama assumed responsibility for police and judicial functions in the Canal Area and for many other services as well. Opinion was nearly unanimous that the new arrangement was satisfactory. Even when U.S. canal employees lost PX, commissary, and APO mail privileges in 1984, many continued to enjoy them through their spouses' employment with the Department of Defense.

The binational canal administration envisioned in the treaty proved more difficult to achieve. At the top, McAuliffe and Manfredo forged a close and constructive partnership that did not appear to suffer with time. McAuliffe handled most liaisons with U.S. agencies, while Manfredo did the same with the Panamanian government. The latter did begin working with the U.S. Congress and other government units in the mid-1980s, with an eye toward succeeding as administrator in 1990. In general, this cooperative spirit prevailed throughout the top echelons of management.

The Panama Review Committee was formed to bring together representatives of various U.S. agencies with interests in the canal and bases. Participants agreed that the committee saw a great deal of constructive decision making that had been absent before the treaties. The embassy, which had historically been a weak member in the "country team," assumed the leadership role.

The Panama Canal Board of Directors, composed of five U.S. and four Panamanian members, did not develop a working basis nearly as easily. At first the Panamanian appointments were thought to be plums that would give access to patronage, which proved untrue. The Panamanian members, moreover, had little staff support from their government and were slow to learn about canal operations. At Manfredo's suggestion, Torrijos had created in 1978 an entity called the Canal Authority. It soon became swamped in bureaucratic fights and jealousies and provided little help to the Panamanian directors. Panamanian board members carried on a debate about ways the Panama Canal Act violated important parts of the treaty; these accusations had much merit, but the act could not be changed and the criticism did not help manage the canal. Most frustrating for the Panamanians was the fact that the House of Representatives had hobbled the commission by forcing it to submit budgets every year and even obliged the U.S. members of the board to vote as instructed by the U.S. secretary of defense. For two years the Board of Directors accomplished very little. Manfredo remarked that the two countries should have held over the treaty negotiating teams to handle these disagreements.

Two changes paved the way for a more effective commission. In 1979 the Panamanian government created a small agency, the Executive Department for Treaty Affairs, to serve solely as staff for Panamanian members of the Board of Directors. This group at first operated within the presidency and then moved permanently to the foreign ministry. Then the railroad and docks (originally to be under the Canal Authority) were taken over by the ports agency. That left the authority with little more than liaison duties and management of the lands returned to Panama. By 1982 the authority ceased to exist, its functions taken over by other agencies. Finally, as the terms of the treaty implementation became known, the Panamanian board members were left more to their own devices and could focus on learning the canal business. Between 1982 and 1985 the Board of Directors functioned fairly smoothly, though it was much weaker than the treaty framers had intended.

Two other bilateral committees—charged with coordinating environmental protection and defense—met fairly often in the early years to map out policy in these areas. The first group produced a Watershed Management Plan and attempted to raise public awareness of the problems of siltation in the canal drainage basin. The defense group and its twenty-six subcommittees worked in the early and mid-1980s to give the National Guard a larger role in canal security.

The Panama Canal Act thwarted the intention of treaty framers by impeding the release of operational profits, from which Panama was to receive up to $10 million a year. Several times canal officials skirted this restriction by transferring budget surpluses to Panama, but this has not occurred recently. Another method of benefiting Panama, at least in the long run, was investment in canal maintenance and improvements. Congress authorized several large capital projects— for example, dredging, locomotive repair shops, lock overhauls, and reconstruction of a hydroelectric plant—so that the canal will be functioning efficiently when it is turned over in 1999. Panama benefits only indirectly from such projects, however, and Congress will likely become stingier as the date of transfer nears.

A new body representing U.S., Panamanian, and Japanese interests —the Tripartite Canal Alternatives Study Group—initiated a series of planning talks during the 1980s to explore new shipping possibilities and to help the canal adapt to changing commercial practices. Officials placed a high priority on widening the Gaillard Cut to accommodate two-way transits of wide beam ships—which make up a growing share of the canal's traffic.

Panamanian planners, in the meantime, discussed the possibility of turning the isthmus into a "centerport," or marshaling point for container cargo. In this conception, world commerce will eventually be fully containerized and funneled through a dozen or so center-ports, where containers will be transferred between ships and trains. A Panamanian centerport would cost some $30 billion to $40 billion, probably only a tenth the cost of a sea-level canal. By the late 1980s, however, this option appeared to have closed due to political conditions in the republic.

Panamanians differ among themselves regarding the success of treaty implementation. Some, especially in the business community, would like the United States to maintain an indefinite presence; leftists and nationalists want the shortest tenure possible. Depending on their views, they prefer greater U.S. supervision (as under the Panama Canal Act) or more autonomy (through the treaty). The foreign ministry continued to object to violations of the treaty, but the State Department did not acknowledge them. Most Panamanians, however, are disappointed at the modest financial rewards that accrue to Panama, which they partly blame for the poor economic performance in the 1980s. And most would like to see the military bases dismantled upon expiration of the SOFA.[4]

In sum, the canal continued to be a successful and profitable enterprise under the joint management created by the new treaties. Those who predicted failure for the arrangement were proven wrong, as were those who expected the canal to be obsolete by the 1980s. It will certainly remain a valuable maritime passage into the next century, though some modernization will have to be undertaken. After the first years of shakedown administration under the new treaties, canal operations receded into the background of U.S.-Panamanian relations.

## Economic Relations in the 1980s

Panama's poor economic performance in the 1980s (Gross Domestic Product [GDP] rose at 3.3 percent a year from 1980 to 1983, just slightly ahead of population growth) was due to both domestic and U.S. decisions. Panama has received much more in cash transfers from the canal—approximately $60 million a year—than it did prior to 1980. In addition, many of the businesses that operated in the former Canal

Zone now pay taxes and fees in Panama and contribute to the nation's GDP. On the other hand, foreign aid to Panama fell to a trickle because of congressional displeasure with the new treaties. So the widespread expectations of a posttreaty boom did not materialize.

On the domestic side, two policies account for much of the 1980s stagnation: previous reliance on debt financing and expensive social programs. Torrijos had availed himself of foreign loans throughout the 1970s to generate and sustain popular support during the lean years of treaty negotiations, a policy Washington did little to discourage. As a result, by the early 1980s Panama had the highest per capita foreign debt in the world and ranked third in Latin America in total indebtedness. Service on the debt drained money from potential investments. In an attempt to win backing for his regime, Torrijos had been generous to workers in his 1972 labor code. He also instituted price controls and subsidies to aid the working class. He invested heavily in health and education programs that provided employment for the middle class and the promise of upward mobility for the poor. In this area he emulated both the Cuban Revolution and the Peruvian military regime of General Velasco Alvarado (1968–75).[5]

Undeniably, some of Torrijos's achievements were impressive: by 1980 literacy stood at 87 percent and life expectancy at seventy-one years. Wage and tax policies created greater equality in the distribution of income. To keep unemployment down, the government put tens of thousands of persons on its payroll and paid for them with borrowed funds. The economy grew at respectable rates (4.7 percent per annum between 1970 and 1975 and 6.3 percent from 1975 to 1980), but most of the increase was in the public sector and in exports of services (trade and international banking). The long-term effects of Torrijos's policies were a huge demand for skilled and white-collar jobs coupled with falling investment in businesses that hired in these sectors. By the early 1980s, the private sector had stagnated, the public sector was bloated, and the masses of people expected good jobs and a much higher standard of living because of the canal. It was not an encouraging situation.[6]

U.S. aid to Panama, generous during the 1970s, plummeted in the following decade. In 1980, for example, it fell to virtually nothing: $2 million for development and $300,000 for military assistance. In the next four years, aid picked up a little, to averages of about $11 million and $4 million, respectively, a sign of Washington's efforts to encourage a transition to democracy after the death of Torrijos in 1981 and to professionalize (and win influence with) the National Guard. Partly in recognition of the desired shift in military orientation, the force was renamed the Panamanian Defense Forces (PDF) in 1983.

In 1985, however, economic and military aid soared to $112 and $27 million, respectively. These increases had several causes. First, the embassy wished to lend a helping hand to Nicolás "Nicky" Ardito Barletta, a University of Georgia-trained economist and a friend of the United States who had become president the year before. Many in the government knew and trusted him and believed he could solve Panama's economic problems. Second, CIA and national security advisers had close relations with the Panamanian military, which they used to channel weapons and supplies (illegal after the congressional ban in 1984) to the Contras in Nicaragua. The military aid was designed in part to reward the general and his staff. Third, the Kissinger Commission of 1983 had recommended committing substantial foreign aid to friendly countries in Central America, as a way to implement the 1981 Caribbean Basin Initiative.

The USAID development program encouraged private initiative and elimination of government controls, together with a general International Monetary Fund austerity effort. This included debt reduction; reduction of public sector employment; privatization of state-owned businesses; and decontrol of agricultural markets. As for emphases, USAID specialists believed that agriculture and industry for export ought to be pushed, rather than services and production for domestic markets. Finally, USAID supported a modest program of low-income housing construction as a way to stimulate the building materials industry.[7]

Little foreign aid actually made its way into Panama's accounts after 1986, however, due to deteriorating relations between the two governments. Panama was left off the list of Central American countries eligible for assistance under the Caribbean Basin Initiative due to the overthrow of President Barletta the previous year. The USAID mission came perilously close to shutting down, a situation that persisted for several more years.

## Political Relations

After the death of Torrijos in 1981, President Royo found himself beset by rivals and out of favor with the National Guard leadership. The commander of the guard, Colonel Florencio Flórez, who preferred that the military remain behind the scenes, was forced into early retirement in March 1982 and replaced by Rubén Darío Paredes. Shortly afterward, the new commander forced Royo to resign. Vice-President Ricardo de la Espriella then became president. Paredes himself stepped down in late 1983 in order to run for president, but it soon became clear that he would lose so he exited the political stage. In this way General Manuel Antonio Noriega became commander of the guard in August 1983, which he renamed the Panama Defense Forces (PDF) the following month.[8]

Noriega was born in 1934 in a Panama City slum, the illegitimate son of an accountant and his maid, who gave him up for adoption to a schoolteacher when Noriega was five. He attended the National Institute, a model public high school, but could not afford to fulfill his career aspiration to become a doctor. Instead he received a scholarship to attend the Peruvian Military Academy, where he graduated in engineering in 1962. When the military turned out Arias in 1968, he held the rank of lieutenant and was already a paid informant for the CIA. In the 1969 countercoup against Torrijos, Noriega, then commander of the garrison in Chiriqui province, sided with Torrijos and put his troops at his disposal. The following year he became head of G-2, the military intelligence service that supplied virtually all secret information for the government and conducted antisubversive activities.

Noriega's involvement in narcotics trafficking—the guard had been involved in the heroin trade from the late forties—commenced shortly. In 1972 it became clear to U.S. officials that he was the Panamanian connection. A high U.S. drug official proposed to President Nixon that the White House "plumbers" assassinate him, but Nixon demurred. For the next decade Noriega served as chief of security, enforcer, and troubleshooter for Torrijos, who once introduced Noriega as "my gangster."[9]

⌈In one instance Noriega failed to serve his U.S. friends.⌉ It was, perhaps, a harbinger of future difficulties. One of the 1977 treaties provided for deactivation of a number of military facilities five years after entering into force. But the Pentagon did not relinquish Fort Gulick, home of the School of the Americas. Since its establishment in 1946 the school had processed tens of thousands of Latin American officers, thus helping to create an inter-American military fraternity. In 1983 U.S. authorities proposed that Noriega sponsor a separate SOFA to guarantee the Pentagon's lease on Fort Gulick, and the general was inclined to do so. Such an agreement, however, would have been extremely unpopular in Panama—the 1926 and 1947 agreements had been rejected by the National Assembly because of widespread protests against expanded military presence. Noriega tarried until 1984 to make a decision. By then, frustrated Pentagon officers had decided to move the school to Fort Benning, Georgia.

Panama's 1984 presidential election provided an opportunity to shift power back to civilian authorities and to improve relations between the two countries. The White House gave heavy backing to Nicolás Ardito Barletta, the U.S.-trained economist who had participated in treaty negotiations and then served as a vice-president of the World Bank. Among other qualifications, his stance against the Contadora peace talks coincided with U.S. preferences. His chief rival was Arnulfo Arias, the eighty-three-year-old former president and a successful populist. Arias, far better known and liked by the masses, led Ardito Barletta in the polls and won the balloting in May 1984. The government, with the knowledge of the embassy, seized ballot boxes, rewrote the totals, and declared Barletta the winner. Secretary of State George Shultz even traveled to Panama to attend the inauguration, a signal of U.S. blessings for the new government.

Barletta—essentially a technocrat—had little experience in politics and soon found himself floundering. His economic policies emphasized World Bank orthodoxy, which meant stabilization, market forces, unemployment, low tariffs, and reduced public spending. In a short time he managed to alienate virtually all sectors of Panamanian society, to the point that even the embassy admitted that he was a failure as a politician. And he could not assert control over the PDF's officers or its commander, who were deeply involved in various illicit activities.

While civilian authorities muddled along with scant real power, Noriega managed an active program at his PDF headquarters. He and Torrijos had become disillusioned with the Sandinistas in 1980, and soon Noriega began helping the U.S.-sponsored Contras in their guerrilla war against the Managua government. At first this involved airlifting arms and supplies to the Contras and moving cocaine up and down Central America. Predictably Noriega did not take ideological sides: he also bought arms from Cuba and sold them to the leftist guerrillas in El Salvador. He used his friendship with the intelligence chief of Honduras, Col. Torres Arias, to land and take off in that country beginning in 1980. He also kept up his ties with intelligence officials in Managua and Washington. These wide-ranging operations later led to the accusation that Noriega was in fact an intelligence broker with allegiances to no one.[10]

Noriega developed a far more lucrative business representing the Medellín drug cartel of Colombia, which had formed in the early 1980s. Panama had long been a transfer point for narcotics, because of the intensive maritime and (after 1949) air traffic there. Noriega cooperated with the cartel to move some of its drugs to the United States when that market blossomed in the 1980s. Noriega also provided the important service of allowing cash from drug profits to be flown into Panama for deposit and laundering in international banks. The money was then recycled through the state bank of Panama. Some observers estimated that banks processed tens of billions of dollars this way, beyond the scrutiny of U.S. authorities.

Finally, Noriega and his top officers operated a number of other rackets from which they reaped great profits. One involved selling visas, passports, and residence permits to Chinese, Lybians, and Cubans so that they could eventually make their way to the United States. Another was shipping high-tech equipment to Cuba and thence

to circumvent a U.S. ban on such trade. Such military
was not new, of course, only the magnitude of the profits
spiratorial mentality that it fostered among officers in the
and.

Noriega's gunrunning, money laundering, and drug smuggling
were tolerated by the United States in the mid-1980s because of
other services he performed. As chief of Panama's intelligence agency,
Noriega had had face-to-face dealings with Vice-President George
Bush and CIA director William Casey. The U.S. government was
caught in a dilemma, especially when in 1984 Congress banned military aid to the Nicaraguan Contras. The Reagan administration had
launched a campaign against drugs in the 1980s, yet about that time
U.S. officials gained irrefutable evidence of Noriega's participation in
the trade. Yet they decided to use Noriega and his contacts in the
region because he could help keep the Contra campaign alive. This
was all the more important when the White House and the national
security advisers began arranging for private contributions and covert
deals to supply arms to the Contras. When these activities became
public in the U.S. Senate hearings in 1987 of the Iran-Contra scandal, Noriega's role surfaced. In short, the Reagan administration used
Noriega to pursue the Contra campaign despite growing evidence of
his own criminal activities.[11]

In August 1985 Noriega became irritated with Barletta, who pressured him to reduce graft in the PDF and allowed a disconcerting
amount of freedom of speech, press, and assembly. The mounting
opposition movement certainly caused the PDF some discomfort too.
The following month, Noriega committed an act that hastened Panama's drift toward open dictatorship. He ordered the assassination
of a leading opposition figure, Hugo Spadafora, who had begun to
publicize Noriega's role in the drug trade. A physician, Spadafora belonged to a prominent family and had become something of a hero
for having commanded a volunteer brigade in the Sandinista revolution of 1979. His grisly murder and decapitation led to public outrage
and clamor for an investigation. When Barletta announced an inquiry,
Noriega's chief of staff, Colonel Roberto Díaz Herrera, forced him to

resign. Vice-President Eric Delvalle became puppet head of state. The U.S. ambassador and other officials wanted to support Barletta against Noriega, but Assistant Secretary of State Elliot Abrams reportedly overruled them.[12]

Two U.S. departments most intimately concerned with Panama policies, State and Defense, went in different directions in the early 1980s and unwittingly created a conflict between civilian and military leadership there. State worked for a civilian, democratic regime in Panama that could honor the treaties and wean the country from its unhealthy dependence on the canal. Defense pumped money, training, and weapons into the PDF in the hope that it would assume more responsibility for protecting the canal. This, it was hoped, would occupy its attention sufficiently to discourage meddling in politics. No one counted, however, on the rising influence of the ambitious, unscrupulous, and wily Noriega, who had promoted himself to general after assuming command. Believing he was in good graces at the White House, Noriega built a machine of repression and crime to enrich himself and his cronies. By the time opposition arose, the machine seemed capable of defying all attempts by Panamanians and Americans to dismantle it.

In retrospect, the United States bore a responsibility for Panama's shift to militarism. Certainly, its tolerance of Noriega's criminal activities in the interest of national security was questionable. But U.S. culpability in Panama's collapse into authoritarian government in the 1980s began in 1968, when Washington's professed determination to promote civilian, democratic regimes in Panama weakened in the wake of the military coup. A decade later, U.S. policy seemed to be driven by the Senate's concern over the security of the canal. At the time, a stable Panama was more critical than a democratic Panama. This meant, among other things, greater involvement by the Panamanian military in the country's domestic politics.

# 9    The Noriega Crisis
and Bush's Ordeal

The discovery of Hugo Spadafora's decapitated, mutilated body in September 1985 horrified observers and set into motion events that led four years later to the most dangerous crisis in the history of U.S.-Panamanian relations. For many Panamanians, the brutal murder was the first indisputable evidence that Noriega was a psychopath and murderer. For Americans, it raised the specter of a monster created by naive U.S. policies designed to safeguard the Panama Canal. From that date, efforts by Panamanians and Americans to curb Noriega's power and force his removal merely fortified his resolve to stay in office and exercise dictatorial power. When the White House finally decided that he should step down, Noriega retrenched, convinced that his only hope for survival lay in preserving his command over the PDF. Finally, it took twenty-four thousand American troops to drive him from office, and in the process Panama became an occupied country, much as it had been in the early years of this century.

## The Making of a Dictator

Nicky Barletta's decision to investigate the Spadafora murder prompted Noriega to replace him with vice-president Eric Delvalle. The technocrat departed Panama for the safety of the United States. Washington looked on with a certain distaste but acquiesced, mostly because Barletta had made such a mess of things and Noriega had seemed trustworthy during his long years of association with U.S. authorities. (Noriega had attended seven military training programs in the old Canal Zone.) He also kept the peace, paramount for the security of the canal, and held decorations from a dozen countries around

154

the world. Assistant Secretary of State Elliot Abrams led the group pledged to keep Noriega in power.

Not everyone concurred with the U.S. decision to support Noriega, however. Panamanian students, journalists, and politicians began to protest the illegal regime, and Noriega applied the usual pressure to silence them. Miguel Antonio Bernal, an impassioned patriot and democrat, tried to mount an opposition movement in Panama City during the summer of 1986 using the radio and opposition press. Military authorities warned Bernal that he was risking his own life and that of his young son, so friends and relatives the following year convinced him to leave the country. For the next three years he published an underground weekly, *Alternativa*, in which he attacked Noriega incessantly. In Panama, censorship and progovernment propaganda invaded the media. A pall fell over U.S.-Panamanian relations.[1]

In mid-1986 a few U.S. public officials and the *New York Times* publicly accused General Noriega of criminal activities. In part this was due to the June 1986 decision by Congress to allow the CIA to resume arms supplies to the Nicaraguan Contras. Noriega's help was no longer critical; indeed, his activities had become an embarrassment to the Reagan administration. In several articles in the *New York Times*, Seymour Hersch detailed allegations of the dictator's role in drug trafficking, gunrunning, spying, and money laundering. Afterward, Noriega's support among U.S. officials rapidly declined. Congress, the State Department, the Justice Department, and the White House favored removal of Noriega; the CIA, Department of Defense, and the Drug Enforcement Agency wanted to keep him in power. A former analyst for the State Department intelligence service described the Noriega dilemma, "It's been my . . . experience with [Panama] that one of the major problems that we have is . . . mixed signals."[2] Still, it was one thing for some officials to voice their belief that Noriega should be removed from power; it was quite another to mobilize enough force to accomplish that goal.

Senator Jesse Helms of North Carolina created the worst trouble for General Noriega by using his position on the Senate Foreign Relations Committee to investigate and publicize all of the accusations against the Panamanian strongman. In the United States, this attack seriously damaged Noriega's image and made it uncomfortable for any government official to defend him. These charges reverberated for months in the world press, generating pressure on the Reagan administration to "do something" about Noriega.[3] In Panama, however, Noriega labeled the attacks a ploy whose ultimate goal was to abrogate the 1977 treaties and prevent the turnover of the canal. He staged patriotic demonstrations against U.S. meddling in Panama's internal affairs and posed as defender of the nation's sovereignty. These affairs did not, however, represent genuine popular support for the regime.[4]

In June 1987 a feud over succession broke out between General Noriega and his chief of staff, Roberto Díaz Herrera. Díaz had reportedly tried to force Noriega to resign, and Noriega decided to "resign" him instead. He offered Díaz the Tokyo embassy (a major source of bribe money) and a million dollars in cash, terms that reflected the powerful position Díaz had occupied for the past several years. Díaz pondered his defeat for a time and then decided to bare his soul—and Noriega's—to the world. He announced that all of the allegations of the previous year were true, and he provided details and embellishments that only an insider would know. He also blamed Noriega for the deaths of Torrijos and Spadafora. The Díaz confessions encouraged the opposition to organize huge demonstrations to demand that Noriega step down. Leaders from important sectors of society, including the Council of Bishops and nearly three hundred professional, educational, and business associations, formed the National Civil Crusade to coordinate marches and protests. In mid-June and late July they declared general strikes that shut down 90 percent of the country's businesses and schools.

Noriega responded by wielding force against the leaders of the crusade. Many were victims of imprisonment, intimidation, and beatings. Demonstrators adopted tactics such as banging empty pots, honking car horns, and waving white handkerchiefs. Noriega threw his riot police—called Dobermans—against the protesters, who rallied almost daily throughout June and July. One participant called it "fifty nights of horror—a war different from the others we knew but still a war, with all the risks and dangers. . . . we fought with handkerchiefs and white flags. They opposed us with force, repression, and lies."[5] Never before in Panama's history had the comfortable middle class mobilized such a campaign, and for a time these protests were a nightly feature of U.S. television news.

When the U.S. Congress passed resolutions favoring elections and civilian government in Panama, Noriega had gangs attack the embassy, consulate, and information service buildings. This brought a protest and demand for restitution, as well as a suspension of aid. The U.S. government, with a resolve that now seemed to signal White House commitment, took a number of steps to show that it backed the opposition and wanted to see Noriega step down. The strategy was to encourage other PDF officers to overthrow Noriega, so that the situation would still be under PDF control rather than in the hands of the people. Yet no one stepped forward, either out of fear of Noriega or concurrence with his policies. By the end of July, almost two months into the protest, Noriega decided to shut down the crusade. He jailed leaders, closed down newspapers and radio stations, and sent an assault squad to take over Díaz's home, where the opposition often met. Díaz was captured and jailed. Many others fled the country. The United States deplored the attack and criticized Noriega but did little else; Díaz himself was released and soon went into exile.

With the loss of leadership and the effectiveness of police terrorism, the protests became more sporadic. General strikes called in August and October failed. The U.S. Congress continued to investigate Noriega's drug and intelligence operations and proclaimed the desirability of a civilian government in Panama. Under pressure from Congress, Reagan eliminated Panama's sugar quota and closed the AID offices in December 1987. Noriega and his supporters, meanwhile, attacked U.S. policies as a destabilization campaign and declared themselves as the defenders of national sovereignty.

In late 1987 representatives of the two governments held secret discussions in order to arrange Noriega's departure from the government. Their aim was to have him leave within three months so that parties and candidates could organize effectively for the May

1989 presidential election. Among other things, this would permit the next president to confer with U.S. officials about the appointment of a Panamanian administrator for the canal in 1990. Perhaps more important was Noriega's removal before the 1988 U.S. presidential election campaign got under way. Associates argued that the dictator had secret documents proving the complicity of U.S. officials in drug smuggling and money laundering in Central America. They implicated the national security staff and the vice-president as well. Such statements proved disconcerting to administration officials on the eve of primary elections. Later, as they feared, Senator Robert Dole, a Republican challenger, did in fact accuse Vice-President Bush of laxity in dealing with Noriega.[6]

Noriega's spokesman in the talks, José Blandón, had been the general's personal aide and intelligence adviser. In January 1988, however, Noriega broke off the talks and disavowed Blandón, who remained in the United States in de facto exile. Blandón and a number of others testified to several congressional committees, receiving wide press coverage. Later he testified before a grand jury.

## The Campaign for Noriega's Removal

In early February 1988 the Justice Department filed numerous indictments against General Noriega in federal courts in Tampa and Miami, alleging that he had participated in the drug trade through Panama. This put more heat on Noriega and indicated that Reagan was getting tough with the general. In point of fact, no sure extradition procedure existed to carry out the indictments. They were apparently filed to send a stronger warning to Noriega.[7] In late February the Reagan administration took another step against Noriega by decertifying Panama for international borrowing, due to its lack of cooperation with antinarcotics activities.

In February the Reagan administration dispatched Assistant Secretary Abrams to Miami to meet with and persuade Delvalle to fire General Noriega.[8] Noriega refused to step down and instead appointed

Manuel Solís Palma to be the next puppet. Delvalle stayed in his home for several days, hoping to generate enough support to force Noriega out. When that failed and he deemed the situation dangerous, he took refuge in a foreign embassy and eventually went into hiding. The U.S. government continued to recognize Delvalle and beginning on March 1 enacted a number of economic sanctions against Panama. Meanwhile, a coup attempt on March 16 was put down.

For the next month Abrams (who had defended the general against attacks less than four years before) headed a campaign to force Noriega's resignation. Washington cut off Panama Canal payments, suspended trade preferences, held up international bank transfers, barred U.S. companies in Panama from paying local taxes, and created a cash-flow crisis by stopping shipments of dollars, Panama's currency. Impounded funds were deposited in escrow for the deposed Delvalle government. Those sanctions remained in effect through the end of 1989, when the escrow account held over $110 million.

Though some economic sanctions continued for nearly two years, they failed to bring down Noriega, as did other attempts to ease him out by negotiation. Big U.S. companies operating in Panama were allowed to pay taxes to avoid being shut down. Japan, Libya, and Mexico advanced loans to Noriega, and the international banks managed to conduct business as usual. Secret negotiations between the two countries in May produced an agreement for Noriega to leave the country in exchange for canceling the indictments against him, but Noriega soon reneged. The Reagan administration, meanwhile, succeeded in keeping the Panama crisis out of the presidential election, and in November Vice-President George Bush defeated Massachusetts Governor Michael Dukakis. Skeptics argued that the Reagan-Bush team merely wished to buy time and avoid a flare-up in Panama and that Noriega was bound to prevail.

In March 1989, for the third successive year, the opposition organized demonstrations to demand the restoration of civil liberties and free elections. The May 1989 presidential contest in Panama provoked a smaller crisis, one of the first to command President Bush's attention. General Noriega had declined to run for president, and his decision may have been based on opinion polls that showed he had a high disapproval rating. He and the regime supported the scion of an elite family, Carlos Duque, to be the next puppet. The opposition nominated for President Guillermo Endara of the Panameñista party, a figure active for many years but without a following of his own. He was joined by veteran Ricardo Arias Calderón and newcomer Guillermo Ford, candidates for vice-president. The freedoms of press, speech, and assembly remained curtailed.

White House officials apparently decided that the election provided another opportunity to pressure Noriega into resigning or at least to embarrass him internationally. They reportedly channeled $10 million into the opposition campaign and focused a great deal of attention on the contest. Former President Jimmy Carter and other dignitaries went to Panama to act as monitors. Based on pre-election surveys and Church-conducted exit polls, the opposition claimed a 75 percent victory, but Noriega had the PDF confiscate hundreds of ballot boxes and otherwise rig the election for his candidate. The foreign monitors denounced the fraud, and the opposition mounted new demonstrations and a general strike. As in 1987, U.S. national television carried scenes of repression against the protesters, including a physical attack on the candidates themselves. The protests subsided in several days, and Noriega declared the election void.

President Bush criticized the cancellation and vowed to continue the economic sanctions. He also sent nineteen hundred troops to join the ten thousand servicemen stationed in Panama. Since 1987 the PDF had harassed U.S. military personnel in Panama, and during the summer a number of fresh incidents occurred between soldiers of the two countries. These included infiltration of U.S. bases at night, provocation of guards, and sniping. The Pentagon seemed at last to abandon its opposition to a direct attack on Noriega by appointing a new chief of the Southern Command. The tension and flare-ups were bad for morale and endangered security, and the twenty thousand or so American civilians living in Panama now constituted a potential hostage population. The long deterioration of U.S.-Panamanian relations accelerated.

The Organization of American States, meanwhile, took up the issue of canceled elections in mid-1989, hoping to defuse the crisis and induce movement toward democracy in Panama. Public opinion in the hemisphere seemed to run against Noriega, yet the U.S. campaign against the dictator was described as a throwback to the days of gunboat diplomacy and interventionism. This effort at diplomatic mediation failed when the OAS issued a mild plea for Noriega to call new elections but stopped short of recommending his ouster.

On 1 September 1989, Noriega installed a personal friend, Francisco Rodríguez, as provisional president and intimated that if relations with the United States improved he might hold new elections for the presidency. Bush took the gesture as an opportunity to escalate the campaign against Noriega. The United States broke diplomatic relations and instituted new economic sanctions. Bush, once Noriega's contact in the Reagan administration, had to distance himself even more from the dictator because he was about to launch a highly publicized "war against drugs." Moreover, the security and efficiency of the canal depended upon finding a Panamanian administrator for the Canal Commission before the 1 January 1990 expiration of the incumbent administrator's term.

The CIA, Southern Command, and other U.S. agencies in touch with the PDF had openly encouraged military leaders to overthrow Noriega and thereby end the crisis. By October the economic constraints imposed by the United States—which had triggered a sharp drop in national income—caused the PDF to miss a payroll. Noriega appeared doomed. A major coup took place on 3 October, with foreknowledge and approval of the United States. Led by Major Moisés Giraldi, commander of the Panama City police, the rebels captured the PDF headquarters and attacked Noriega's car with a fusillade of bullets when it entered the courtyard. Noriega survived and was held captive all morning by the leaders of the coup. U.S. forces, meanwhile, blocked some roads that loyalists might have taken to save the general, and they overflew the PDF headquarters in helicopters. At a critical juncture, however, U.S. agents fumbled an attempt to receive Noriega into their custody. Soon a loyalist battalion routed the rebels and arrested their officers. When Noriega restored his personal command, he ordered the executions of three dozen conspirators and reportedly shot several himself. President Bush and Secretary of Defense Dick Cheney came in for sharp criticism for their failure to give more support to the coup.

Noriega seemed more entrenched than ever. He had resisted pressure to resign from both Reagan and Bush, weathered conspiracies and demonstrations, and had not faltered. For Bush, however, Noriega was a monster whose provocative words and acts brought discredit and ridicule upon the president. The United States appeared unable to take decisive action, in part because the Pentagon regarded the large U.S.-citizen population there a hostage to any Panamanian threat of violence. Only a full-scale evacuation of noncombat U.S. personnel from Panama would enable the United States to force Noriega's removal, and such a move would have unpredictable consequences for the future of the canal and U.S. bases there.

Although the crisis of late 1989 took the form of a duel between Noriega and Bush, it was driven in part by the schedule of the 1977 treaty. Noriega's nomination of Carlos Duque (reputedly Noriega's bag-man for illegal money) as administrator was ignored by the United States, which in turn pushed for the deputy administrator, Fernando Manfredo, who had been groomed for the job. As a stopgap, the United States announced that it would appoint Manfredo as interim administrator when the incumbent stepped down. Panama's delegates, as they had since January 1988, continued to boycott meetings of the Board of Directors. U.S. authorities believed that American prestige depended upon an orderly, dignified process of treaty implementation. That was clearly impossible with Noriega in power.

One final aspect of the crisis was the poor marks President Bush was receiving for his international policies in late 1989. Only a month after the Chinese government crushed prodemocracy demonstrations, he had secretly sent emissaries to Beijing, a move unpopular with the American public. He also appeared overcautious by not giving more support to the anticommunist upheavals in Eastern Europe, surely one of the most favorable developments in the previous thirty years.

In comparison, Premier Mikhail Gorbachev had won widespread acclaim for his statesmanlike handling of Eastern Europe and for helping to end the cold war. In these circumstances, Bush's image of inaction (the so-called wimp factor) was aggravated by Noriega's continued control of Panama.

## The Christmas Invasion

Following the failed coup of October, U.S. military authorities drew up plans for an invasion to topple Noriega, disperse the PDF, and safeguard U.S. citizens and property in Panama.[9] Noriega, meanwhile, strengthened his civilian militias (called the Dignity Battalions) and also continued to challenge Bush, mostly to bolster his nationalistic image at home. By December an irresistible force faced an immovable object.

On 15 December, Noriega's subservient and extraconstitutional National Assembly of Counties named him Panama's chief of government, just as its predecessor had done for Omar Torrijos in 1972. Noriega then declared that for the past thirty months the United States, "through constant psychological and military harassment, has created a state of war in Panama." He then criticized President Bush and urged his countrymen to resist, though not militarily. He also castigated Bush for violating the terms of the treaty, which he claimed to uphold to the letter of the law, and stated that "we would never destroy the canal." The last was true. Noriega did not threaten the canal or declare war on the United States, as the U.S. media reported.[10]

The incident that triggered the invasion occurred the following night, when several U.S. soldiers in a jeep drove by PDF headquarters and were fired upon. One soldier died from his wounds. During the next two days U.S. and Panamanian authorities traded accusations and occasionally gunfire, while preparations for the invasion—code-named Operation Just Cause—went forward.

The United States moved thousands of troops from Fort Bragg and several Stealth fighters (F-117s) from California to Fort Clayton in Panama. In the early morning hours of 20 December U.S. forces attacked a number of PDF installations, including the headquarters in Panama City, the Rio Hato base, and Tocumen airport. The total number of U.S. forces approached twenty-four thousand, and they employed airborne transport, fighters, tanks, mortars, and light armored vehicles. Within a short time the headquarters and much of the surrounding tenement district were destroyed, and most of the other installations were under U.S. control.[11] General Noriega, however, had been at an officers club on the outskirts of the city and managed to escape into hiding. The United States posted a $1 million reward for his capture and set about trying to establish order, paying cash bounties for weapons turned in voluntarily.

Just before the invasion U.S. authorities brought together the three opposition candidates in the 7 May elections—Endara, Arias Calderón, and Ford—and arranged for a secret swearing-in ceremony. As soon as press representatives could be brought in, they were shown videotapes of the ceremony, by way of presenting the new government, patently a creation of the United States. The U.S. recognized Endara and appointed as ambassador Dean Hinton, a troubleshooter adept at liaison between the White House and Congress but hardly an international diplomat. At the same time, U.S. agents attempted to seize Noriega's assets, thought to be worth $30 million to $60 million, on the grounds that they were obtained illegally. Finally, U.S. authorities pledged that reconstruction aid would mount into the billions of dollars, to overcome the effects of the invasion and economic sanctions.

For the next four days fighting continued in and around Panama City as U.S. troops met resistance from remnants of the PDF and the Dignity Battalions. Normal police activity ceased, and looters took over the commercial districts of downtown Panama. U.S. casualties climbed into the hundreds, while perhaps a thousand Panamanians were killed. Military censors withheld accurate information for weeks. Meanwhile the Pentagon termed the invasion a complete success, "the most surgical operation of its size ever carried out," implicitly contrasting it to the mistake-riddled invasion of Grenada six years earlier.

The American public seemed to agree, for polls showed overwhelming approval of the president's actions.

On 24 December Noriega and other members of his high command took refuge in the papal nunciature. U.S. forces had kept the Cuban and Nicaraguan embassies under close surveillance to prevent him from entering but did not watch the Vatican premises.[12] This set off a week-and-a-half ordeal for the nuncio and his staff, who by long tradition had to protect Noriega but who were gravely discomforted by his presence and the pressure for his release brought to bear by the United States. The puzzle had many elements: the Vatican rarely turned over persons in diplomatic asylum, the Endara government could not guarantee Noriega's safety and prosecution in Panama, the Bush administration wanted to try Noriega in U.S. courts, Panama and the United States had no clear procedures for extradition, and irregularities in Noriega's imprisonment might lead to a mistrial. Time worked on Bush's side, however, for after nine days and much urging by the papal nuncio, Noriega surrendered to U.S. authorities and was taken to Miami for arraignment.

The Noriega crisis ended in early January 1990, but the long job of rebuilding Panama and restoring sovereignty had only begun. Although the U.S. commander there spoke of his "nation-building" efforts, in reality only the Panamanians could accomplish the task; indeed, the presence of an occupying army would hinder progress toward that goal. It had taken Panama's earlier generations decades to consolidate nationhood, always using the United States as a foil. Now they would have to do so during the final years of U.S. withdrawal under the 1977 treaty. Panamanian reactions to the invasion were overwhelmingly in favor, according to a Gallup Poll, and persons interviewed by the press expressed jubilation over Noriega's fall and their rescue by the United States. Still, no one sought out those who might be opposed and intimidated. Doubtless, the longer the troops occupied Panama the greater would be the resentment against them. A lingering question concerned whether the State Department would recover some of its influence over relations with Panama after the Pentagon had commanded the invasion and mopping-up operations.

International opinion makers deplored the invasion as a violation of international law and procedures, even though some heads-of-state expressed sympathy for Bush's dilemma. The UN and the OAS condemned the U.S. action, and virtually all observers expressed a desire for an early departure of the nonpermanent U.S. forces. Many also feared the possibility of the United States returning to the policies of gunboat diplomacy in the hemisphere. One critic wrote, "I don't see that devastating a small country's economy, then mounting a 25,000-man invasion which kills more than 300 people and wounds hundreds more, to seize a disreputable but unimportant military adventurer over whom American courts have disputed jurisdiction, should be considered a success."[13]

The canal, reopened after a brief suspension of transits for security reasons, did not appear to have been in danger either before or during the invasion. The Endara government agreed to the interim appointment of Fernando Manfredo as commission administrator, and the canal went back to business as usual. U.S. troops withdrew from Panamanian territory in early February 1990.

## The Aftermath

Eventually we may come to regard the Noriega crisis as another of the casualties of the Contra war in Nicaragua, since that effort led the Reagan administration to strengthen the PDF and to accept Noriega as dictator in the mid-1980s. It will probably also be seen, in the long view, as the Bush administration's effort to clean up a mess of its own creation in order to deal more effectively with the portentous developments in Eastern Europe. As long as Noriega could thumb his nose at the United States and claim special status because of his CIA connections, Bush could hardly occupy high moral ground in his dealings with the rest of the world. But such conclusions must await the release of classified documents, the publication of memoirs, and the luxury of more hindsight.

As for U.S.-Panamanian relations at the personal level, the invasion is certain to produce dependency relationships among officials and a distancing among ordinary citizens. The invasion seems to confirm what many leftists have stated (and rightists hoped) over the years— Panama is not really a sovereign state and ultimately the United States will have its way there by force. President Endara conveyed that mood in an unguarded interview with an Associated Press correspondent: the invasion was "like a kick in the head. It was not the best thing I would have thought. . . . We were not really consulted. . . . I would have been happier without an intervention. . . . The gringos have their defects, but I am used to . . . them." All thoughtful Panamanians will be having similar thoughts for years to come.

To be sure, the Panamanian economy began to rebound with emergency aid expenditures, and the administration sent Congress a request for a billion-dollar reconstruction program. This represented approximately $500 for every man, woman, and child and begged comparison with Peter Sellers's comedy, *The Mouse that Roared*, in which a small country declared war on the United States in order to receive bounteous reparations payments afterward. Congress stalled for many months and approved less than half the original amount, so it is unlikely that aid will pull Panama back into the U.S. orbit. In the long run Panama will continue its economic drift toward Japan, whose investments in large-scale transit projects will probably supplant U.S. assets.

The implementation of the 1977 treaties should proceed on course, since that was a major rationale for the drive to oust Noriega and ultimately invade Panama. Manfredo will probably continue the policies of McAuliffe, who sought to maintain the operating efficiency of the canal until 1999. Canal management will continue training and placing Panamanians in managerial and skilled jobs. Finally, Manfredo must try to assume effective command over the huge canal bureaucracy in an environment of American hegemony.

The most important choice facing U.S. and Panamanian authorities is whether to reassemble an army in the image of the PDF or to replace it with a police force, such as Panama had until the 1950s and Costa Rica has had since that time. Reports of U.S. recruitment of some 80 percent of the former PDF officers into a new force raised fears that an army would be created—one led, moreover, by some of yesterday's oppressors. In addition, by February 1990 the PDF was back up to fourteen thousand troops. Thus Endara's government faces restraints on its authority from two sources: the United States and its own military.

# Epilogue

The Christmas 1989 invasion marked a watershed in U.S.– Panamanian relations and served as metaphor for the legacy of bonds fashioned over 170 years. Ties between Panama and the United States constituted an alliance, one based upon a symbiotic relationship. The partnership took shape in the decades leading up to the opening of the railroad and became permanent once the canal treaty was signed. The symbiotic quality came from the fact that the alliance satisfied basic national aspirations of both countries: the U.S. goal of building and controlling a transit facility in Central America and the Panamanian dream of becoming an international center for trade and services. Because the canal still serves these purposes, it continues to bind the two countries together.

But the alliance conflicted with other national aspirations of the two countries, and in this regard the railroad and canal created powerful tensions between them. To be sure, Panamanians experienced the tension more, because the canal loomed so large in their history, whereas Americans tended to take it for granted and to derive pride from many other sources. Panama's citizens wanted to make their country into a genuine nation-state, respected in the international arena and able to conduct its own domestic affairs. The treaties authorizing the railroad and canal provided for U.S. maintenance of order and hence limited Panama's sovereignty. In this sense they were intolerable to nationalists, even though they did turn Panama into a crossroads of the world.

For the United States, the alliance also contained a contradiction, though not as obvious or painful as Panama's. From Washington's presidency until the 1940s, the republic revered the principle of no entangling alliances, yet the railroad and canal constituted just that. Moreover, Americans liked to believe that their country's foreign policies helped to spread peace, democracy, and prosperity abroad.

America stood for an "empire of freedom." Repeated protests from Panama raised troubling doubts about the beneficence of the U.S. presence. Its tutelary role—policing, observing elections, advising presidents, giving aid, and occasionally intervening—were proof that we had *not* created a truly independent Panama. Then when the United States gave up many of those activities, the instability of Panama's politics and economy seemed to mock the idea that our presence somehow wrought positive effects.

Another problematic aspect of the U.S.-Panamanian alliance was the degree to which both sides desired or opposed Americanization of the isthmus. The huge U.S. enterprise and bases could not help but encourage Panamanians to become more like the gringos: they spoke English more and better than any other Latin peoples except Puerto Ricans; they shared many U.S. business and work ethics; and their arts and leisure activities incorporated much U.S. popular culture. Yet Panamanians lamented this deculturation and tried to recover and strengthen what they regarded as their Hispanic heritage. Arnulfo Arias's frequent successes at the polls proved the appeal of this nationalistic sentiment, which he called Panameñismo. Yet many Panamanian leaders sought—consciously or not—to promote Americanization as a way to achieve progress. Panama's patriots rejected U.S. culture and values on principle yet longed to share the American way of life.

U.S. citizens also had mixed feelings about the Americanization of Panama. Most regarded it as the best and perhaps only hope for local progress. They dispensed advice on how to do things "the American way" for a century and a half. They promoted Panamanians who worked for the canal or bases using criteria from the United States: mastery of English, work ethics, cleanliness, affability, and productivity. Still, Americans could not go so far as to annex Panama, symbolically or actually. In their view America did not practice colonialism, acquire territory, oppress nonwhite peoples, or exploit an unequal relationship. So Americans believed that the United States and Panama enjoyed a partnership beneficial to both. Indeed, many Americans in Panama forged close friendships and even intermarried with Panamanians. Some also pursued local studies of archaeology, botany, geology, history, and other subjects, thereby validating their importance. In this way they affirmed their belief in the legitimacy of the Panamanian nation-state and its alliance with the United States.

The Christmas invasion of 1989 etched these dilemmas and contradictions in high relief and foreshadowed difficult relations in the 1990s. Panamanians are caught in a sovereignty-prosperity bind (they do not seem ever to coincide in time), and Americans seem to be trapped between the desires to do the right thing (treat Panama as a nation-state) and to guarantee that the canal continues to operate efficiently through 1999. The invasion blasted the myth that the partnership was mutually beneficial and began the final countdown to the moment when it will dissolve altogether. For better or worse, the U.S.-Panamanian alliance of 140 years is coming to an end.

# Notes

## Introduction

1. Quoted in John Major, "The Panama Canal Zone, 1904–1979," in *Cambridge History of Latin America*, vol. 7, ed. Leslie Bethell (Cambridge, Eng., 1990), 663.

## 1. Independence and Early Relations

1. W. Davidson Weatherhead, *An Account of the Late Expedition against the Isthmus of Darien* (London, 1821), 22–68; Alex Perez-Venero, *Before the Five Frontiers: Panama from 1821–1903* (New York, 1978), 2 and n. 5; and Celestino Andrés Araúz, *La independencia de Panamá en 1821* (Panama City, 1980), 83.
2. Alfredo Figueroa Navarro, *Dominio y sociedad en el Panamá colombiano: 1821–1903* (Panama, 1978), 51–54; E. Taylor Parks, *Colombia and the United States, 1765–1934* (Durham, N.C., 1935), chap. 5.
3. Araúz, *Independencia de Panamá*, 40–67, passim.
4. Ibid., 68–89, passim; Perez-Venero, *Five Frontiers*, 2–4.
5. Figueroa, *Dominio y sociedad*, 138–39.
6. Araúz, *Independencia de Panamá*, pp. 97–98. The regulation is published in Celestino A. Araúz and Jorge Kam Ríos, "Relaciones entre Panamá y los Estados Unidos de América (siglo xix)," *Boletín de la Academia Panameña de la Historia*, nos. 5–6 (October 1975–March 1976): 105–13.
7. Arthur Preston Whitaker, *The United States and the Independence of Latin America, 1800–1830*, 2d ed. (New York, 1964), chap. 13; Lester D. Langley, *America and the Americas* (Athens, Ga., 1989), 40–48; Parks, *Colombia and the United States*, 101–3.
8. Eduardo Lemaitre Román, *Panamá y su separación de Colombia*, 2d ed. (Bogota, 1972), 55–56. John J. Johnson, "United States–British Rivalry in Latin America, 1815–1830: A Reassessment," *Jarbuch fur Geschischte von Staat, Wirtschaft unde Gesellschaft Lateinamerikas* 22 (1985): 341–91, argues

that the strategic rivalry has been overestimated and that trade dominated each country's priorities.

9. Whitaker, *United States and Independence,* chap. 19; Langley, *America and the Americas,* 49–52; Parks, *Colombia and the United States,* 137–47. Congress's delay resulted from Southerners' fear that an antislavery resolution might arise, a desire by Jackson's followers to embarrass Adams, and reluctance to join military alliances with the Latin republics. See Ralph Sanders, "Congressional Reaction in the United States to the Panama Congress of 1826," *The Americas* 11 (1954): 141–54.

10. Jackson Crowell, "The United States and a Central American Canal: 1869–1877," *Hispanic American Historical Review* 49 (1969): 34; Harmodio Arias, *The Panama Canal* (London, 1911), 10–14; Araúz and Kam, "Relaciones," pp. 51–54.

11. Perez-Venero, *Five Frontiers,* 8–9; Baltasar Isaza Calderón and Carlos Alberto Mendoza, *La constitución boliviana de 1826 y sus deplorables consecuencias* (Panama, 1983).

12. Figueroa, *Dominio y sociedad,* 138–45.

13. Perez-Venero, *Five Frontiers,* 13–15.

14. Ibid., 190–93; Figueroa, *Dominio y sociedad,* 28–68, 221–24, 234–37, and chap. 6, passim; Perez-Venero, *Five Frontiers,* 31–34.

15. Perez-Venero, *Five Frontiers,* 39–42, 108; Figueroa, *Dominio y sociedad,* 33–35.

16. Gerstle Mack, *The Land Divided* (New York, 1944), chap. 11.

17. The most complete account is Robert A. Naylor, *Penny Ante Imperialism: The Mosquito Shore and the Bay of Honduras, 1600–1914* (Rutherford, N.J., 1989).

18. Perez-Venero, *Five Frontiers,* 53–54; Parks, *Colombia and the United States,* 185–90.

19. Mack, *Land Divided,* chap. 12.

20. Naylor, *Penny Ante Imperialism,* chaps. 12–14; Mary Wilhelmine Williams, *Anglo-American Isthmian Diplomacy, 1815–1915* (Washington D.C., 1916), 30–31.

21. Mark J. Van Aken, "British Policy Considerations in Central America before 1850," *Hispanic American Historical Review* 42 (1962): 54–59; Langley, *America and the Americas,* 71–81.

22. On U.S. economic disinterest in the region, see Parks, *Colombia and the United States,* chap. 10. The urge to possess the California coast is covered

by Norman A. Graebner, *Empire on the Pacific* (New York, 1955). William H. Goetzmann, *When the Eagle Screamed* (New York, 1966), chap. 6, argues for a romantic American dream of worldwide empire.

23. Goetzmann, *Eagle Screamed*, 35–37 and chap. 3, passim.

24. Robert R. Russel, *Improvement of Communication with the Pacific Coast as an Issue in American Politics, 1783–1864* (Cedar Rapids, Iowa, 1948), chaps. 1–2; Langley, *America and the Americas*, 57–70.

25. Ibid., pp. 76–77; Naylor, *Penny Ante Imperialism*, chaps. 15–16; Williams, *Anglo-American* (1916), 52–53.

26. See Mack, *Land Divided*, chap. 19.

27. John Haskell Kemble, *The Panama Route, 1848–1869* (Berkeley and Los Angeles, 1943), 1–3. Mack, *Land Divided*, part 1, provides a good background of the colonial transit experience.

28. Kemble, *Panama Route*, 8–13, quoted from p. 200. On the navy in Caribbean diplomacy, see Lester D. Langley, *The Banana Wars*, 2d ed. (Chicago, 1985), introd.

29. Kemble, *Panama Route*, 16.

30. Parks, *Colombia and the United States*, chap. 12; Perez-Venero, *Five Frontiers*, 55–58; Mack, *Land Divided*, 132–35; Araúz and Kam, "Relaciones," 60–73; Lemaitre, *Panamá y su separación*, 53–61.

31. William Paul McGreevey, *An Economic History of Colombia, 1845–1930* (Cambridge, Eng., 1971), chap. 4.

32. Parks, *Colombia and the United States*, 200–207.

33. Ibid., 207–10.

34. Ibid., 219–24.

35. Figueroa, *Dominio y sociedad*, 261.

36. Naylor, *Penny Ante Imperialism*, chap. 15; Goetzmann, *Eagle Screamed*, 78–81.

37. Williams, *Anglo-American* (1916), chap. 3, passim; Mack, *Land Divided*, 179–87.

38. Naylor, *Penny Ante Imperialism*, chap. 15.

39. Goetzman, *Eagle Screamed*, 82. Naylor, *Penny Ante Imperialism*, chap. 16, sees the British accomplishment as more modest.

40. Williams, *Anglo-American*, chaps. 4–9, covers the stormy life of the Clayton-Bulwer Treaty. For Panamanian views, see Araúz and Kam, "Relaciones," 73–79.

## 2. The Railroad Era

1. Figueroa, *Dominio y sociedad*, 261.
2. Kemble, *Panama Route*, 22–23; Mack, *Land Divided*, chaps. 13–14, passim. A popular account is Joseph L. Schott, *Rails across Panama* (Indianapolis, 1967).
3. Olive Senior, "The Panama Railway," *Jamaica Journal* 14 (1980): 66–77.
4. Schott, *Rails across Panama*, 139, 191–92.
5. Ibid., 63.
6. Ibid., 151–52.
7. Figueroa, *Dominio y sociedad*, 292–93.
8. Parks, *Colombia and the United States*, 279.
9. Figueroa, *Dominio y sociedad* 280, 289–91.
10. Schott, *Rails across Panama*, 192.
11. Ibid., 205–6.
12. Mack, *Land Divided*, 435–36.
13. Ibid., chap. 17; Schott, *Rails across Panama*, chap. 6; Kemble, *Panama Route*, chap. 3.
14. Kemble, *Panama Route*, 81–94, passim.
15. Joseph Freehof, *America y el título del canal* (Bogota, 1916), cited in Lemaitre, *Panamá y su separación*, 90.
16. Williams, *Anglo-American Isthmian Diplomacy, 1815–1915*, 2d ed. (Gloucester, Mass., 1965), 233–38.
17. Kemble, *Panama Route*, 254–55.
18. Ibid., 110–14, 207–8.
19. Perez-Venero, *Five Frontiers*, chap. 4.
20. Parks, *Colombia and the United States*, 219–21.
21. Perez-Venero, *Five Frontiers*, 87.
22. Figueroa, *Dominio y sociedad*, 265, 310–16.
23. Compare the remarks of Justo Arosemena before and after the railroad, quoted in Araúz and Kam, "Relaciones," 74–76.
24. Figueroa, *Dominio y sociedad*, 273, 278, 302–8.
25. The proposal is reprinted in William R. Manning, ed., *Diplomatic Correspondence of the United States: Inter-American Affairs, 1831–1860*, vol. 5 (Washington, D.C., 1935), 399–403, n. 1.
26. Mack, *Land Divided*, 161–65; quoted from 164–65. On the incident see also Figueroa, *Dominio y sociedad*, 339–42; Perez-Venero, *Five Frontiers*, 98–103;

Schott, *Rails across Panama*, 193–99; Parks, *Colombia and the United States*, 221–24. On the claims negotiations, see ibid., chaps. 18–19.

27. Justo Arosemena and Gil Colunje, *Teoria de la nacionalidad*, 2d ed. (Panama City, 1968).

28. Mack, *Land Divided*, 158–60; Parks, *Colombia and the United States*, 228–30.

29. Perez-Venero, *Five Frontiers*, 91.

## 3. The French Period

1. Jackson Crowell, "The United States and a Central American Canal: 1869–1877," *Hispanic American Historical Review* 49 (1969): 27, 35. On Grant's expansionist tendencies, see Walter LaFeber, *The New Empire* (Ithaca, N.Y., 1963), 32–39.

2. Parks, *Colombia and the United States*, 338–39.

3. Ibid., 345–50; Lemaitre Román, *Panamá y su separación*, 92–97; Mack, *Land Divided*, 166–67. The second treaty was more favorable to the United States than the first. They are discussed together merely to highlight new arrangements contemplated by Grant and Seward.

4. Williams, *Anglo-American* (1965), 273–74; quoted from 274.

5. Parks, *Colombia and the United States*, 346–47.

6. See Miles P. Duval, *Cadiz to Cathay*, 2d ed. (Stanford, Calif., 1947), appendix k, for a list of the commissions and boards formed.

7. Crowell, "Central American Canal," 36–39.

8. Parks, *Colombia and the United States*, chap. 22.

9. Mack, *Land Divided*, 168–70.

10. Ibid., part 3; David McCullough, *The Path between the Seas* (New York, 1977), book 1; Joseph Bucklin Bishop, "The French at Panama," *Scribner's Magazine* 53 (January–June 1913): 25–45.

11. Quoted from Williams, *Anglo-American* (1965), 275. Cf. Walter E. Lowrie, "France, the United States, and the Lesseps Panama Canal: Renewed Rivalry in the Western Hemisphere, 1879–1889" (Ph.D. diss., Syracuse University, 1975); Parks, *Colombia and the United States*, chap. 23; Lemaitre, *Panama y su separación*, 245–46; Araúz and Kam, "Relaciones," 85–86.

12. *Land Divided*, 308–9.

13. Ibid., 315–16.

14. Ibid., 275–86, passim.

15. Williams, *Anglo-American*, 278.

16. Omar Jaen Suárez, *La población del istmo de Panama del siglo xvi al siglo xx* (Panama City, 1978), 530–39.

17. Figueroa, *Dominio y sociedad*, 349–51.

18. The best discussion of migration statistics is Velma Newton, *The Silver Men: West Indian Labour Migration to Panama, 1850–1914* (Kingston, Jamaica, 1984), chap. 5. On Africans, see Gary G. Kuhn, "Liberian Contract Labor in Panama, 1887–1897," *Liberian Studies Journal* 6 (1975): 43–52.

19. An excellent introduction to the subject is John and Mavis Biesanz, *The People of Panama* (New York, 1955). On sociopolitical conflict, see Alfredo Figueroa Navarro, "Tensiones sociales en el arrabal (1850–1880)," *Tareas* 39 (1977): 5–13.

20. Perez-Venero, *Five Frontiers*, chap. 5, passim.

21. See the commemorative volume about Prestán, *Boletín de la Academia Panameña de Historia (BAPH)* 41 (May–June 1985), and Jorge Luis Macías, "Hacia una reevaluación de la figura de Pedro Prestán," *BAPH* 46–47 (January–June 1986): 15–38.

22. Perez-Venero, *Five Frontiers*, 115. Mack, *Land Divided*, 352, mentions 740 troops.

23. Admiral J. G. Walker to Commander Bowman McCalla, 6 Apr. 1885, document 2E, file ZE (Panama, Panama Canal), Naval History Center, Washington, D.C., Naval Yard; Daniel Wicks, "Dress Rehearsal: United States Intervention on the Isthmus of Panama, 1885," *Pacific Historical Review* 49 (1980): 581–605.

24. Cf. Mack, *Land Divided*, 350–54.

25. Figueroa, *Dominio y sociedad*, 351–52; Ernesto J. Castillero Reyes, *La historia de Panamá*, 8th ed. (Panama City, 1982), 146–47.

26. Mack, *Land Divided*, 346–50, and McCullough, *Path between the Seas*, 159–60, discuss official figures. The figure twenty thousand is based on the later chief U.S. medical officer's estimate that mortality was three times the officially stated total. See William Gorgas to George W. Goethals, 9 Oct. 1912, Goethals papers, Library of Congress Manuscript Collection.

27. Mack, *Land Divided*, chap. 30.

28. Michael L. Conniff, *Black Labor on a White Canal: Panama, 1904–1981* (Pittsburgh, 1985), chaps. 1–2.

29. Mack, *Land Divided*, chap. 18.

30. Williams, *Anglo-American* (1965), 287.

31. On the 1890s, see Parks, *Colombia and the United States*, chap. 24.

32. James M. Skinner, *France and Panama: The Unknown Years, 1894–1908* (New York, 1989), 41–43.
33. Ibid., chap. 3.
34. Ibid., chap. 4.
35. Ibid., 107.
36. Mack, *Land Divided*, 419.
37. Skinner, *France and Panama*, 157–63.
38. The literature on American imperialism is vast. Two interpretations that emphasize the Latin American region are LaFeber, *New Empire*, and David Healy, *U.S. Expansionism* (Madison, Wis., 1970). Healy's more recent book, *Drive to Hegemony: The United States in the Caribbean, 1898–1917* (Madison, Wis., 1988), devotes chap. 5 to the Panama Canal.
39. Mack, *Land Divided*, 421–22.
40. The standard biography is Arthur H. Dean, *William Nelson Cromwell* (New York, 1957).
41. Mack, *Land Divided*, 417.
42. Ibid., 435–36.
43. DuVal, *Cadiz to Cathay*, reprints the Spooner Act in appendix g.
44. Williams, *Anglo-American (1965)*, 288.
45. McCullough, *Path between the Seas*, 256–59.
46. Ibid., chap. 10. On the U.S. press treatment, see Soon Jin Kim, "An Anatomy of the Hearst Press Campaign to Fortify an American Isthmian Canal" (Ph.D. diss., University of Maryland/College Park, 1982).
47. McGreevey, *Economic History*, 87–88.
48. Perez-Venero, *Five Frontiers*, 121. Pp. 129–54 provide a good account of the war in Panama.
49. Ibid., 144.
50. Lemaitre, *Panamá y su separación*, 432–37.
51. Perez-Venero, *Five Frontiers*, 156–57.
52. Ibid., 158.

## 4. Canal Diplomacy, 1902–1919

1. Healy, *Drive to Hegemony*, provides a fine overview.
2. Parks, *Colombia and the United States*, 1935, 411–12.
3. Rolando Ernesto Hernandez Solis, "1903 en la historiografía de la República" (graduation thesis, University of Panama, 1977), chap. 1.

4. The indispensable sources are John Major, "Who Wrote the Hay–Bunau-Varilla Convetion?" *Diplomatic History* 8 (1984): 115–23; Charles D. Ameringer, "Philippe Bunau-Varilla: New Light on the Panama Canal Treaty," *Hispanic American Historical Review* 46 (1966): 28–52; and Charles D. Ameringer, "The Panama Canal Lobby of Philippe Bunau-Varilla and William Nelson Cromwell," *American Historical Review* 68 (April 1963): 346–63. Mack, *Land Divided*, and DuVal, *Cadiz to Cathay*, among others, also provide thorough accounts.

5. According to Hay-Herrán, the treaty would be renewable at the sole discretion of the United States. The stipulation of a one-hundred-year period, however, created an opportunity for Colombia to renegotiate the terms.

6. William McCain, *The United States and the Republic of Panama* (Durham, N.C., 1937), chap. 2.

7. Parks, *Colombia and the United States*, chaps. 26–27, passim.

8. A sample of the highly nationalistic attitudes of Americans is Ray Stannard Baker, "The Glory of Panama," *American Magazine* 76 (November 1913): 33–37.

9. One of the best descriptions of the physical operation of the canal is chap. 21 of McCullough, *Path between the Seas*.

10. The best account of Canal Zone history is John Major, "The Panama Canal Zone, 1904–1979," *Cambridge History of Latin America*, vol. 7, ed. Leslie Bethel (Cambridge, Eng., 1990), 643–70.

11. Goethals to Judson, 21 June 1912, Goethals papers, Library of Congress Manuscript Collection. Cf. Joseph Bucklin Bishop, "A Benevolent Despotism," *Scribner's Magazine* 53 (January–June 1913): 303–19.

12. Gustavo A. Mellander, *United States in Panamanian Politics: The Intriguing Formative Years* (Danville, Ill., 1971), 50–54; Baltasar Isaza Calderón, *Carlos A. Mendoza y su generación* (Panama City, 1982), 295.

13. William F. Sands, *Our Jungle Diplomacy* (Chapel Hill, N.C., 1944), 16.

14. McCullough, *Path between the Seas*, chap. 15; Joseph Le Prince, *Mosquito Control in Panama* (New York, 1916).

15. William Howard Taft, *The Physical, Political, and International Value of the Panama Canal*, 2d ed. (Albuquerque, N.Mex., 1979), 22.

16. McCain, *United States and the Republic of Panama*, chap. 3.

17. Sands, *Jungle Diplomacy*, 48–51; Harry A. Franck, *Zone Policeman 88* (New York, 1913), 145.

18. Norman J. Padelford, *The Panama Canal in Peace and War* (New York, 1942),

chap. 4; U.S. Army, *History of the Panama Canal Department*, 4 vols. (Quarry Heights, C.Z., 1947).

19. Wayne D. Bray, *The Common Law Zone in Panama* (San Juan, Puerto Rico, 1977); Lawrence O. Ealy, *Yanqui Politics and the Isthmian Canal* (University Park, Pa., 1971), chap. 9.

20. A fine account of this process is contained in part 1 of Herbert and Mary Knapp, *Red, White, and Blue Paradise: The American Canal Zone in Panama* (New York, 1984).

21. Mellander, *United States in Panamanian Politics*, 80–86, passim; McCain, *United States and the Republic of Panama*, chap. 4.

22. See Conniff, *Black Labor*, 41–42; Isaza, *Carlos A. Mendoza*, chap. 21. I am grateful to James Howe for sharing portions of Marsh's personnel file that document the incident.

23. McCain, *United States and the Republic of Panama*, chap. 5. U.S. troops did land in the Coto region in 1921 to prevent Panama's attempt to retake the disputed territory.

24. George W. Baker, "The Wilson Administration and Panama, 1913–1921," *Journal of Inter-American Studies* 8 (April 1966): 291.

25. Thomas M. Leonard, "The Commissary Issue in American-Panamanian Relations, 1900–1936," *The Americas* 30 (1973): 83–87.

26. See Conniff, *Black Labor*, chap. 3.

27. Franck, *Zone Policeman*, 29.

28. The classic on UFCO is Charles David Kepner, Jr., *Social Aspects of the Banana Industry* (New York, 1936), esp. chap. 3. The Panamanian point of view is provided by Humberto E. Ricord et al., *Panama y la frutera* (Panama City, 1974), chap. 1. A recent ethnographic treatment is Philippe I. Bourgois, *Ethnicity at Work: Divided Labor on a Central American Banana Plantation* (Baltimore, 1989), chaps. 1–2.

29. McCain, *United States and the Republic of Panama*, 99ff.

30. Mallet to Grey, 22 Aug. 1910, Foreign Office Papers 371/944/33140, Public Records Office, London.

31. Baker, "Wilson Administration," 289.

32. Ricardo Alfaro, "Medio siglo de relaciones entre Panamá y los Estados Unidos," *Panamá, 50 años de república* (Panama City, 1953), 128.

33. Cited in Steve C. Ropp, *Panamanian Politics: From Guarded Nation to National Guard* (New York, 1982), 35.

34. See Michael L. Conniff, "Panama Since 1903," *Cambridge History of Latin America*, vol. 7, ed. Leslie Bethell (Cambridge, Eng., 1990), 603–5, 614–15.

35. Sands, *Jungle Diplomacy*, 68.
36. For a summary account, see Lawrence O. Ealy, *The Republic of Panama in World Affairs, 1903–1950* (Philadelphia, 1951).

## 5. From Gunboats to the Nuclear Age, 1920–1945

1. Celestino Andrés Araúz, "Belisario Porras y las relaciones de Panamá con los Estados Unidos," *Cuadernos Universitarios* 3 (1988): 13–16.
2. In 1921 President Porras asked for troops to break up demonstrations against him for his stance on the border conflict with Costa Rica (McCain, *The United States and the Republic of Panama*, 207–8). On the 1920 strike and President Chiari's appeal for help in dealing with a rent strike in 1925, see Conniff, *Black Labor*, 56–61, 65.
3. Manuel Octavio Sisnett, *Belisario Porras o la vocación de la nacionalidad* (Panama City, 1959), 288–89.
4. McCain, *United States and the Republic of Panama*, chaps. 6, 10; Sisnett, *Belisario Porras*, 243–45, 291–305.
5. Thomas M. Leonard, "The United States and Panama: Negotiating the Aborted 1926 Treaty," *Mid-America* 61 (Oct. 1979): 189–203; McCain, *United States and the Republic of Panama*, chap. 11; J. Conte Porras, *Arnulfo Arias Madrid* (Panama City, 1980), 63–68; Alfaro, "Medio Siglo," 132–34.
6. Major, "Panama Canal Zone," 650, suggests that State helped approve private loans to the Panamanian government in order to facilitate negotiation of the 1926 treaty.
7. J. G. South to SD, 13 March 1925, G-2 Regional Files for Latin America, 1933–1944, Panama, RG165, USNA; James Howe, "Native Rebellion and U.S. Intervention in Central America," *CS Quarterly* 10 (1986): 59–65. For the texts, see Carlos Manuel Gasteazoro, Celestino Andrés Araúz, and Armando Muñoz Pinzón, eds., *La historia de Panamá en sus textos* (Panama City, 1980), 2:88–112.
8. Hernando Franco Muñoz, *Movimiento obrero panameño, 1914–1921* (Panama City, 1979), 36–37 and 32–45, passim; Conniff, *Black Labor*, pp. 63–64.
9. On the 1930s see McCain, *United States and the Republic of Panama*, chap. 12; Almon R. Wright, "The United States and Panama, 1933–1949," U.S. Department of State Research Project 499, 1952, part 1; John Major, "F.D.R. and Panama," *Historical Journal* 28 (1985): 357–77; and Conniff, *Black Labor*, chap. 5.

10. The coup is covered in Conte, *Arnulfo*, 68–78, 193–96; Gasteazoro et al., *Textos*, 2:119–24; Davis to Secretary of State, 6 Jan. 1931, in G-2 Regional Files for Latin America, 1933–1944, Panama, RG165, USNA.

11. Edgar B. Nixon, ed., *Franklin D. Roosevelt and Foreign Affairs*, vol. 1 (Cambridge, Mass.: 1969), 419.

12. Lester D. Langley, "Negotiating New Treaties with Panama, 1936," *Hispanic American Historical Review* 48 (May 1968): 220–33, and "The World Crisis and the Good Neighbor Policy in Panama, 1936–1941," *The Americas* 24 (1967): 137–52.

13. A good demographic portrait of the Zone population is A. Grenfell Price, "White Settlement in the Panama Canal Zone," *Geographical Review* 25 (January 1935): 1–11.

14. The minutes of the negotiations are in 711.1928/436 1/2, State Department Decimal File, 1930–39, RG 59, USNA. Alfaro's summary is in "Medio siglo," 134–37; Wright's, 57–66.

15. "Political Trends in Panama, 1931 to November, 1943," 24 January 1944, G-2 Regional files for Latin America, 1933–44, Panama, RG 165, USNA.

16. Donald Allan Yerxa, "The United States Navy and the Caribbean Sea, 1914–1941" (Ph.D. diss., University of Maine, 1982); John Andrew Cooley, "The United States and the Panama Canal, 1938–1947" (Ph.D. diss., Ohio State University, 1972). On the 1939 Panama meeting, see David G. Haglund, *Latin America and the Transformation of U.S. Strategic Thought, 1936–1940* (Albuquerque, N.Mex., 1984), 148–52. For an overview, see Stetson Conn and Byron Fairchild, *The Western Hemisphere: The Framework of Hemisphere Defense* (Washington, D.C., 1960).

17. Wright, "United States and Panama," 83–109; Padelford, *Panama Canal*, chap. 4. On naval defenses, see "Historical Report of Formation and Workings of Panama Sea Frontier," 7 Dec. 1944, Strategic Plans Division, NG6, Panama Sea Frontier, box 201, Naval History Center, Washington, D.C.

18. On Arnulfo's controversial first administration, see Conte, *Arnulfo*, 90–101 passim.

19. Wright, "United States and Panama," 110–36.

20. Ibid., 137–58; Undated (ca. June 1942) report of internments, G-2 Regional Files for Latin America, 1933–44, Panama, RG 165, USNA.

21. John Major, "Wasting Asset: The U.S. Re-Assessment of the Panama Canal, 1945–1949," *Journal of Strategic Studies* 3 (September 1980): 124.

22. For labor import figures, see Rubén Carles, Jr., *La evolución de la política de*

*empleo y salarios en la zona del canal y el desarrollo económico de Panamá* (San Pedro Sula, Honduras, 1970), 51–53.

23. Francisco Herrera, "El aporte americano a la universidad," *Revista Loteria* 354–55 (1985): 152–62. Examples of publications resulting from these exchanges are John and Mavis Biesanz, *The People of Panama* (New York, 1955) and the *Boletín del Instituto de Investigaciones Sociales y Económicas.*

24. These events are covered in John Major, " 'Pro mundi beneficio'? The Panama Canal as an International Issue, 1943–8," *Review of International Studies* 9 (1983): 17–34, and Conniff, *Black Labor,* 101–3. Cf. also Paul Blanchard, *Democracy and Empire in the Caribbean* (New York, 1947).

## 6. Uneasy Partners, 1945–1960

1. George Brett to Chief of Staff, U.S. Army, 18 May 1944, and to Adjutant General, U.S. Army, in Operations and Plans Division, 336, Panama, RG 165, USNA. See also Wright, "United States and Panama," part 3.

2. Major's " 'Pro mundi beneficio'?" is indispensable here. Quote from Paul Blanchard, *Democracy and Empire in the Caribbean* (New York, 1947), 203.

3. See Conniff, *Black Labor,* chap. 6, esp. 112–17; Wright, "United States and Panama," 267–82. For an overview of labor in the canal, see Serafino Romualdi, *Presidents and Peons: Recollections of a Labor Ambassador in Latin America* (New York, 1967), chap. 7.

4. See, for example, J. Parnell Thomas, "Reds in the Panama Canal Zone," *Liberty* (May 1948), 15–54.

5. The best account is John Major, "Wasting Asset: The U.S. Re-Assessment of the Panama Canal, 1945–1949," *Journal of Strategic Studies* 3 (September 1980): 123–46. A good overview of the era is Thomas M. Leonard, "United States Perception of Panamanian Politics, 1944–1949," *Journal of Third World Studies* 5 (Fall 1988): 112–38.

6. John Major, "The Panama Canal Zone, 1904–1979," *Cambridge History of Latin America,* vol. 7, ed. Leslie Bethell (Cambridge, Eng., 1990).

7. Wright, "United States and Panama," 204–23; Larry LaRae Pippin, *The Remón Era: An Analysis of a Decade of Events in Panama, 1947–1957* (Stanford, Calif., 1964), 9–16; Camilo O. Pérez, *Anatomía de un rechazo* (Panama City, 1974?).

8. Pippin, *Remón Era,* 31–36; Wright, "United States and Panama," 247–56.

9. Wright, "United States and Panama," 229–41, 283–89.

10. Major, "Panama Canal Zone"; Pippin, *Remón Era*, 77–80. An insiders' view of Zone life is Herbert Knapp and Mary Knapp, *Red, White, and Blue Paradise: The American Canal Zone in Panama* (New York, 1985). For the cold war stance on Latin America at this time, see State Department's "Report to the National Security Council on U.S. Policy . . . ," 28 June 1948, NSC, pt. 16, in National Security Council files, RG273, USNA. The legislation was PL 841, approved by the Eighty-first Congress on 26 Sept. 1950.

11. "Conference on Possible Canal Zone Efforts to Alleviate Critical Panamanian Situation," 11 Jan. 1952, 719.00/1-1152, and "Projects to Relieve Unemployment in Panama," 24 Jan. 1952, 719.001/1-2452, RG59, USNA.

12. 9 Feb. 1953, 719.5 MSP/2-953, RG59, USNA.

13. Pippin, *Remón Era*, chap. 1; Biesanz, *People of Panama*, 140–41; Ropp, *Panamanian Politics*, pp. 27–28; quoted from 24 Mar. 1953 memo in the Eisenhower Library, document 1984–1859 in the *Declassified Documents Reference System* (Washington, D.C.), hereafter cited as *DDRS*.

14. Wiley to State, 26 May 1952, 719.00/5-2652, RG59, USNA.

15. Siracusa to Wiley, 11 June 1952, 719.5-MSP/6-1152, RG59; quoted from Wiley to Collins [original underscored], 13 Mar. 1953, CD091.3/Panama, Defense—Executive Office Central Decimal Files, RG330, USNA. For a general discussion of early foreign assistance theory, see Robert Packenham, *Liberal America and the Third World* (Princeton, N.J.: 1973). The anticommunist stance was delineated by the National Security Council, whose recommendations are contained in RG273, USNA.

16. Pippin, *Remón Era*, 95–106.

17. Ropp, *Panamanian Politics*, 28–29.

18. Wiley to Cabot, 19 Mar. 1953, and passim, 719.00/3-1953, RG59, USNA. The best overall account of negotiations is in Pippin, *Remón Era*, chap. 9.

19. Major, "Panama Canal Zone," 657–58.

20. Halaby to Secretary of Defense, 14 Oct. 1953, and enclosed memo from Stevens to Secretary of Defense, CD092/Panama, Defense—Executive Office Central Decimal Files, RG330, USNA.

21. Memo on meeting, 28 Sept. 1953, Eisenhower Library, document 1984-1163, *DDRS*; "NSC Progress Report by Under Secretary of State . . . ," 20 Nov. 1953, NSC144/1, RG273, USNA.

22. Gasteazoro et al., *Textos*, 2:263–80.

23. George Westerman, interview with author, 1982. On ratification, see Pippin, *Remón Era*, 145–50.

24. Pippin, *Remón Era*, 150.

25. Unsigned, undated report in the Eisenhower Library, document 1984–1865, *DDRS*.

26. Lawrence O. Ealy, *Yanqui Politics and the Isthmian Canal* (University Park, Pa., 1971), 116 and chap. 10, passim; Sheldon B. Liss, *The Canal: Aspects of United States-Panamanian Relations* (Notre Dame, Ind., 1967), chap. 3; G. Bernard Noble, *Christian A. Herter* (New York, 1970), p. 206; Herter to Butler, 14 Nov. 1957, Herter Papers, document 1985-105, *DDRS*.

27. On Panama's strategy in this era, see William Anthony Naughton, "Panama Versus the United States: A Case Study in Small State Diplomacy" (Ph.D. diss., American University, 1972).

28. *Panama Tribune*, 17 July 1958, 1; Ealy, *Yanqui Politics*, 84.

29. Milton Eisenhower, *The Wine is Bitter: The United States and Latin America* (Garden City, N.Y., 1963), 225–26. An excellent treatment of the Eisenhower policies in Latin America as a whole is Stephen G. Rabe, *Eisenhower and Latin America: The Foreign Policy of Anticommunism* (Chapel Hill, N.C., Press, 1988).

30. Conniff, *Black Labor*, 119.

31. Gasteazoro et al., *Textos*, 280–87; Intelligence report 19 Aug. 1958, Eisenhower Library, document 1985-2080, *DDRS*; Walter LaFeber, *The Panama Canal: The Crisis in Historical Perspective* (New York, 1979), 121–26. For a history of flag incidents in the Canal Zone, see File 28-B-150, RG 185, Panama Canal Commission Records Center.

32. Conte, *Arnulfo*, 179; Joint Chiefs of Staff, Central File 1959, file CCS 129, Panama 9125/9105, RG218, USNA.

33. Marco A. Gandásegui et al., *Las luchas obreras en Panama, 1850–1978* (Panama City, 1980), 62–64.

34. Liss, *The Canal*, 61–64; after action report on riots of 28 Nov. 1959, Joint Chiefs of Staff, Central File 1959, CCS 129/Panama, file 9125/9108.

35. Meeting of Eisenhower, Milton Eisenhower, and Livingston Merchant, 27 Nov. 1959, Eisenhower Library, document 1985-299, *DDRS*; Noble, *Christian A. Herter*, 207–16, passim.

36. Minutes of Panama Canal Board of Directors Meeting, 9 Apr. 1960, Panama Canal Commission, Agency Records Center; Farland notes on meeting with president, 9 Aug. 1960, Eisenhower Library, document 1984-1164, *DDRS*.

37. Rubottom to Montgomery, 28 June 1960, Eisenhower Library, document 1985-106, *DDRS*; quoted from NSC 5902, RG273, USNA; "Isthmian Canal

Plans—1960," 11 Feb. 1960, in Joint Chiefs of Staff Central File, file 9125/7105, RG218, USNA.

## 7. A Time of Troubles and Treaties, 1960–1979

1. Langley, *America and the Americas,* chaps. 8–9.
2. November 1960 memo in Eisenhower Library, document 1984-2171, *DDRS.*
3. Liss, *The Canal,* 126–35; Ealy, *Yanqui Politics,* 117–19; LaFeber, *Panama Canal,* 132–35.
4. "Consultation with Congressional Committees on Panama Canal Policy," unsigned, undated, Kennedy Library, document 1984-1165, *DDRS.*
5. William J. Jorden, *Panama Odyssey* (Austin, Tex, 1984), 31–34; "Status Report . . . on the President's plan of action," 29 Aug. 1962, and "Minutes of Panama Review Group," 23 Apr. 1963, Kennedy Library, documents 1984-400 and 1984-2581, *DDRS.*
6. Liss, *The Canal,* 117–25.
7. Interview with author, Capt. Paul B. Ryan, and the Robert J. Fleming Jr. Papers, Hoover Institution Archives. For the Pentagon's reluctance to make concessions, see file 9125/9105 [dated 15 Sept. 1961, covering through October 1963] Joint Chiefs of Staff, RG218, USNA. Cf. Conniff, *Black Labor,* 177–79.
8. Interview with Jack Hood Vaughn, 19 Oct. 1990.
9. Many sources are available on the riots: Jorden, *Panama Odyssey,* chap. 3; Ealy, *Yanqui Politics,* chap. 11; U.S. Consulate report, "The Flag Riots: Chronicle of a Crisis," 3 Feb. 1964, Johnson Library, document 1984-401, *DDRS;* and International Commission of Jurists, *Report on the Events in Panama, January 9–12, 1964* (Geneva, 1964).
10. Jorden, *Panama Odyssey,* 64.
11. Ibid., chap. 4.
12. John Elac, interview with author, 26 June 1986.
13. Jack Vaughn, interview with author, 29 Oct. 1990.
14. Jorden, *Panama Odyssey,* chap. 5, contains the fullest printed account of the 1964–67 negotiations. Cf. also the in-house history, "The Department of State during the Administration of President Lyndon B. Johnson, November 1963–January 1969," Johnson Library, document 1985-2081,

*DDRS*. The 2 Dec. 1964 meeting is covered in Johnson Library, document 1986-1035, *DDRS*.

15. Bundy to Johnson, 27 Jan. 1965, Johnson Library, document 1986-988, *DDRS*.

16. Rostow to Johnson, 5 Apr. 1966, Johnson Library, document 1986-1034, *DDRS*.

17. David N. Farnsworth and James W. McKenney, *U.S.-Panama Relations, 1903–1978* (Boulder, Colo., 1983), chap. 3, discuss the multiple pressures that operated in both countries. Psychologist Charles Imig and the author organized the community development program.

18. Interview with author, Lopez Guevara, 23 July 1986; Renato Pereira, *Panamá: Fuerzas armadas y politica* (Panama City, 1979), 100–110; Ropp, *Panamanian Politics*, 36–38; *Panama Election Factbook: May 12, 1968* (Washington, D.C., 1968). For biographical material, see J. Conte, *Arnulfo*, and Jorden, *Panama Odyssey*, 120–27.

19. Ropp, *Panamanian Politics*, chap. 3; Pereira, *Fuerzas armadas*, 110–27; Jorden, *Panama Odyssey*, 127–40. For several years pro-Arnulfo guerrillas in Chiriqui province fought against guard units, resulting an estimated four hundred deaths. Richard M. Koster and Guillermo Sánchez, *In the Time of the Tyrants* (New York, 1990), chap. 2.

20. On the brief Martínez period, see Koster and Sánchez, *Time of the Tyrants*, chap. 3. A good overview of the period is German Muñoz, "Panamanian Political Reality: The Torrijos Years" (Ph.D. diss., University of Miami, 1981).

21. The U.S. government did not take a position on the coup, but some intelligence officers might have encouraged Torrijos, whom they had known for some time. Wayne Bray, interview, 1 Dec. 1989.

22. Pereira, *Fuerzas armadas*, 128–33.

23. Sharon Phillipps, "Labor Policy in an Inclusionary-Authoritarian Regime: Panama under Torrijos" (Ph.D. diss., University of New Mexico, 1987).

24. The best discussion of Torrijos's style and program is Koster and Sánchez, *Time of the Tyrants*, chaps. 4–7. See also LaFeber, *Panama Canal*, 167–74.

25. Ropp, *Panamanian Politics*, esp. chaps. 3–6.

26. Ibid., chap. 7, provides a good overview of the treaty talks and outcomes.

27. Jorden, *Panama Odyssey*, 330–31, 688–89.

28. Ibid., chap. 7; Major, "Panama Canal Zone," 643–70; author's interviews with Carlos López Guevara, 23 July 1986, Juan Antonio Tack, 23 July 1986, and Diogenes de la Rosa, 18 July 1986.

29. Robert E. Looney, *The Economic Development of Panama* (New York, 1976), chap. 7.

30. George Priestly, *Military Government and Popular Participation in Panama* (Boulder, Colo., 1986). A good academic account of these years, Ropp, *Panamanian Politics*, chaps. 4–6, may be supplemented with the more readable and passionate *Time of the Tyrants* by Koster and Sánchez.

31. Jorden, *Panama Odyssey*, chap. 8; interview with author, Juan Antonio Tack, 23 July 1986.

32. Rómulo Escobar Bethancourt, *Torrijos: Colonia americana no!* (Bogotá, 1981), 207. Farnsworth and McKenney, *U.S.-Panama Relations*, chap. 7, describes the Security Council meeting in detail.

33. Jorden, *Panama Odyssey*, chap. 9 and appendix A. Nixon's and Kissinger's disdain for the Panama Canal issue is conveyed by the fact that neither mentioned it in his memoir on this period. William Jorden, appointed to the NSC staff in 1972, handled Latin American affairs and soon became deeply involved in relations with Panama. In early 1974 he became U.S. ambassador to Panama, where he served throughout the final treaty negotiations. His book *Panama Odyssey*, the most complete account of these years in print, shows how he played the discreet role of go-between and facilitator for the frontline negotiators and many other actors involved. See especially chap. 10.

34. A fascinating glimpse of the opposition is available in the Donald Dozer papers at the Hoover Institution. Dozer, a Latin American history professor at the University of California at Santa Barbara who retired in 1972, organized an active letter and newsletter campaign against the 1967 and 1977 treaties and helped recruit Reagan to the cause. He called his organization the Emergency Committee to Save the U.S. Canal Zone. Jorden, *Panama Odyssey*, chap. 13, and Farnsworth and McKenney, *U.S.-Panama Relations*, chap. 9, deal with domestic political opposition to the canal treaty negotiations.

35. Jorden, *Panama Odyssey*, chap. 11. Farnsworth and McKenney, *U.S.-Panama Relations*, chap. 8, provides an overview of the 1974–77 negotiations from the U.S. point of view.

36. Jorden, *Panama Odyssey*, 257–61.

37. Ibid., 268–72.

38. Ibid., chap. 12.

39. See Jimmy Carter, *Keeping Faith: Memoirs of a President* (New York, 1982), 152–85, and Cyrus Vance, *Hard Choices: Critical Years in America's Foreign*

*Policy* (New York, 1983), 140–57.

40. Jorden, *Panama Odyssey*, chap. 14.
41. Ibid., chap. 15; Sol M. Linowitz, *The Making of a Public Man* (Boston, 1985), chap. 7.
42. Jorden, *Panama Odyssey*, chap. 16.
43. Linowitz, *Public Man*, 177. Thomas M. Leonard provides a thoughtful analysis of the treaties in "The 1977 Panama Canal Treaties in Historical Perspective," *Journal of Caribbean Studies* 2 (Autumn-Winter 1981): 190–209.
44. *National Review*, 17 Feb. 1978, 210–17.
45. Jorden, *Panama Odyssey*, 612.
46. Ibid., chap. 17; Linowitz, *Public Man*, chap. 8; Farnsworth and McKenney, *U.S.-Panama Relations*, chaps. 10–11; William L. Furlong and Margaret E. Scranton, *The Dynamics of Foreign Policymaking* (Boulder, Colo., 1984), chap. 5; John Opperman, "The Panama Canal Treaties," in *Legislating Foreign Policy*, eds. Hyt Purvis and Steven J. Baker (Boulder, Colo., 1984), 77–105.
47. This occurred despite the fact that their jobs and privileges were protected under the treaty; many simply did not wish to live in the reconstructed zone, now called the Panama Canal Area.
48. Furlong and Scranton, *Dynamics*, chap. 6.
49. Jorden, *Panama Odyssey*, Epilogue.

## 8. Treaty Implementation, 1979–1985

1. Jorden, *Panama Odyssey*, 683–84; interviews with author, McAuliffe and Manfredo, 22 and 29 July 1986; U.S. Comptroller General, *Report to the Congress: Implementing the Panama Canal Treaty of 1977* (Washington, D.C., 1980); and John P. Augelli, "The Panama Canal Area in Transition," *American Universities Field Staff Reports* nos. 3–4 (1981). Terrence Modglin's authoritative newsletter, *Panama Proceedings* (1981–84), chronicled the implementation from Washington's point of view.
2. PANAMAX is a standard ship size with the maximum dimensions capable of transiting the canal. Much of this account is based upon interviews with senior canal officials and official documents.
3. On labor aspects of the transition see Conniff, *Black Labor*, 152–56.
4. Luis Restrepo Rosas, *History of a Slander* (Panama City, 1987), lists fifty

alleged violations of the treaties. Former negotiator Carlos López Guevara provided a thoughtful assessment of the canal options in his Panama
City Speech at the Universidad Tecnológico, 21 May 1986, "Preservar la
eficiencia y neutralización del canal de Panamá." Cf. also Carlos Bolívar Pedreschi, *De la protección del canal a la militarización del país* (Panama
City, 1987).

5. On the economic policies of the 1970s, see Robert E. Looney, *The Economic
   Development of Panama* (New York, 1976), and Ropp, *Panamanian Politics*,
   chaps. 4–6.

6. For a survey of the country's economy at mid-decade, see World Bank,
   *Panama: Structural Change and Growth Prospects* (Washington, D.C., 1985).

7. *USAID Panama Action Plan*, FY 1987–FY 1988, 4 Apr. 1986.

8. For an overview of the 1980s see Guillermo Sánchez Borbón, "Panama
   Fallen among Thieves," *Harper's*, December 1987, 57–67.

9. Noriega's entry in *Current Biography* (March 1988), 35–38, can be supplemented by his Curriculum Vitae compiled in 1987. Recent accounts of
   Noriega's career and the invasion are John Dinges, *Our Man in Panama*
   (New York, 1990) and Frederick Kempe, *Divorcing the Dictator* (New York,
   1990).

10. This section draws on news reports of congressional hearings on Noriega's
    activities, summarized in Latin American Data Base, *Panama in Crisis:
    1987–1988* (Albuquerque, N.Mex, 1988).

11. John Weeks and Andrew Zimbalist, "The Failure of Intervention in
    Panama: Humiliation in the Backyard," *Third World Quarterly* 11 (January
    1989): 1–27.

12. Guillermo Sánchez Borbón, "Hugo Spadafora's Last Day," *Harper's*, June
    1988, 56–62.

## 9. The Noriega Crisis and Bush's Ordeal

1. Author's interviews with Miguel Antonio Bernal and other Panamanians
   in July 1986.

2. Ambassador Francis McNeil, 4 Apr. 1988, testimony to the Senate Subcommittee on Terrorism, Narcotics, and International Operations.

3. The opposition newspaper, *La Prensa*, reprinted a sampling of these stories
   in its 12 Sept. 1986 edition.

4. I am indebted to Brittmarie Janson Perez for information on the late 1980s from her dissertation research.

5. Personal communication to author from Alfredo Castillero Calvo, 28 July 1987; Sánchez, "Panama Fallen among Thieves," 57–67.

6. Blandón, 4 Apr. 1988, testimony before the Senate Subcommittee on Terrorism, Narcotics, and International Operations. Three very good sources for the overall crisis are Joe Pichirallo and Patrick E. Tyler, "Long Road to the Invasion of Panama," *Washington Post*, 14 Jan. 1990; "Frontline: The Noriega Connection," PBS television, 30 Jan. 1990; and Weeks and Zimbalist, "Failure of Intervention," 1–27.

7. The 1904 and 1977 treaties permitted Panama to turn over criminals to the U.S. judicial system, but the 1986 constitution barred extradition.

8. Delvalle, part owner of a sugar mill, had been hurt financially by the U.S. suspension of the sugar quota.

9. The following account is based heavily on press reports and the Latin American Data Base (LADB) at the University of New Mexico.

10. Foreign Broadcast Information Service, coverage of 15 Dec. 1989.

11. There is strong evidence that the Dignity Battalions, Noriega's civilian militiamen, torched the tenements during the U.S. attack. Interview with author, Brittmarie Jansen Pérez, 13 July 1990.

12. It is possible that the army knew of and allowed Noriega's asylum in the nunciature.

13. William Pfaff, Los Angeles Times Syndicate, 7 Jan. 1990.

# Bibliographical Essay

The most useful access point to the literature on U.S.-Panamanian relations is Wayne Bray's annotated guide, *The Controversy over a New Canal Treaty between the United States and Panama* (Washington, D.C., 1976). For Spanish-language sources see Carlos Manuel Gasteazoro, Celestino Andrés Arauz, and Armando Muñoz Pinzón, eds., *La historia de Panamá en sus textos* (Panama City, 1980), 2:331–448. English titles predominate in Eleanor Langstaff, *Panama* (Oxford and Santa Barbara, Calif., 1982).

Most general works on the United States and Panama focus on the canal. Among the best are David McCullough, *The Path Between the Seas* (New York, 1977); Gerstle Mack, *The Land Divided* (New York, 1944); and Miles DuVal, *Cadiz to Cathay*, 2d ed. (Stanford, Calif., 1947), and *And the Mountains Will Move* (Stanford, Calif., 1947). A competent survey at the time of World War II is Norman J. Padelford, *The Panama Canal in Peace and War* (New York, 1942). John Major's "The Panama Canal Zone, 1904–1979," *Cambridge History of Latin America*, vol. 7, ed. Leslie Bethell (Cambridge, Eng., 1990), 643–70 and his several other fine articles mentioned in the notes provide essential reading, as will his forthcoming book, *Mandate for Civilization*.

The Panamanian side is well represented by Ernesto Castillero Pimentel, *Panamá y los Estados Unidos* (Panama City, 1953), and Ricard J. Alfaro, *Medio siglo de relaciones entre Panamá y los Estados Unidos* (Panama City, 1959). Alfaro's career and beliefs can be sampled in Carlos Manuel Gasteazoro, *El pensamiento de Ricardo J. Alfaro* (Panama City, 1981). The Colombian view predominates in Eduardo Lemaitre Román, *Panamá y su separación de Colombia*, 2d ed. (Bogotá, 1972).

A candid look at intercultural relations in the construction era is contained in Harry A. Franck, *Zone Policeman 88*, 2d ed. (New York, 1970); a similar treatment of the 1960s and 1970s by longtime zone residents is Herbert Knapp and Mary Knapp, *Red, White, and Blue Paradise: The American Canal Zone in Panama* (New York, 1985). Daniel Goldrich, in *Sons of the Establishment* (Chicago, 1966), interviewed university students regarding their attitudes toward the United States in the early 1960s, a critical time in relations.

Broad surveys of U.S.-Panamanian relations include Walter LaFeber, *The*

*Panama Canal: The Crisis in Historical Perspective* (New York, 1979), a new left interpretation, Lawrence O. Ealy, *Yanqui Politics and the Isthmian Canal* (University Park, Pa., 1971), and Sandra W. Meditz and Dennis M. Hanratty, eds., *Panama: A Country Study* (Washington, D.C., 1989). A synthesis of Panama's recent history is Michael L. Conniff, "Panama Since 1903," *Cambridge History of Latin America*, vol. 7, ed. Leslie Bethell (Cambridge, Eng., 1990), 603–42.

For the nineteenth century, see Celestino Andrés Araúz, *La independencia de Panama en 1821* (Panama City, 1980), and Alex Perez-Venero, *Before the Five Frontiers: Panama from 1821–1903* (New York, 1978). Excellent sociopolitical introductions to Panama are Alfredo Figueroa Navarro, *Dominio y sociedad en el Panamá colombiano, 1821–1903* (Panama City, 1978), and Omar Jaen Suárez, *La población del istmo de Panamá del siglo xvi al siglo xx* (Panama City, 1978).

Traditional diplomatic approaches are found in E. Taylor Parks, *Colombia and the United States, 1765–1934* (Durham, N.C., 1935), Mary Wilhelmine Williams, *Anglo-American Isthmian Diplomacy, 1815–1915*, 2d ed. (Gloucester, Mass., 1965), and William McCain, *The United States and the Republic of Panama* (Durham, N.C., 1937). The best account of the British role in Central America is Robert A. Naylor, *Penny Ante Imperialism: The Mosquito Shore and the Bay of Honduras, 1600–1914* (Rutherford, N.J., 1989).

On U.S. expansionism and Panama, see Norman A. Braebner, *Empire on the Pacific* (New York, 1955); William H. Goetzmann, *When the Eagle Screamed* (New York, 1966); Robert R. Russel, *Improvement of Communication with the Pacific Coast as an Issue in American Politics, 1783–1864* (Cedar Rapids, Iowa, 1948); John Haskell Kemble, *The Panama Route, 1848–1869* (Berkeley and Los Angeles, 1943); Walter LaFeber, *The New Empire* (Ithaca, N.Y., 1963); and Joseph L. Schott, *Rails across Panama* (Indianapolis, 1967). The recent book by David Healy, *Drive to Hegemony* (Madison, Wis., 1988), chap. 5, puts Panama into the wider perspective of the Caribbean during the years 1898 to 1917. Richard H. Collin's *Theodore Roosevelt's Caribbean: The Panama Canal, the Monroe Doctrine, and the Latin American Context* (Baton Rouge, La., 1990) deals exhaustively with presidential actions in Panama and in the region.

Economic relations in general are covered in Robert E. Looney, *The Economic Development of Panama* (New York, 1976), while the World Bank's *Panama: Structural Change and Growth Prospects* (Washington, D.C., 1985) deals with domestic issues. A candid look at the banana industry appears in Philippe I. Bourgois's *Ethnicity at Work: Divided Labor on a Central American Banana Plantation* (Baltimore, 1989), a timely addition to Charles David Kepner, Jr., *Social Aspects of the Banana Industry* (New York, 1936).

The canal diplomacy that led to the 1903 treaty has been dealt with by hundreds of authors, including most of the books listed above. Charles D. Ameringer's works penetrate the deepest: "The Panama Canal Lobby of Philippe Bunau-Varilla and William Nelson Cromwell," *American Historical Review* 68 (1963): 346–63, and "Philippe Bunau-Varilla: New Light on the Panama Canal Treaty," *Hispanic American Historical Review* 46 (1966): 28–52.

On labor migrations and cultural interaction, see Velma Newton, *The Silver Men: West Indian Labour Migration to Panama, 1850–1914* (Kingston, Jamaica, 1984), and Michael L. Conniff, *Black Labor on a White Canal: Panama, 1904–1981* (Pittsburgh, 1985). Bonham C. Richardson's *Panama Money in Barbados, 1900–1920* (Knoxville, Tenn., 1985) treats the migrations and their impact on the West Indies. John and Mavis Biesanz, *The People of Panama* (New York, 1955), provide the best portrait and analysis of mid-century Panamanian society (including relations with Americans) of any book available. Alfredo Castillero Calvo's *La sociedad panamena* (Panama City, 1970) is less ambitious but insightful. On the role of Panama's Indians see Bourgois's book cited above and James How, "Native Rebellion and US Intervention in Central America," *CS Quarterly* 10 (1986): 59–65. On the Watermelon Riot incident, see Mercedes Chen Daley's "The Watermelon Riot: Cultural Encounters in Panama City, April 15, 1856," *Hispanic American Historical Review* 70 (1990), 85–108.

James M. Skinner, *France and Panama: The Unknown Years, 1894–1908* (New York, 1989), covers the New Panama Canal Company. Gustavo A. Mellander, *United States in Panamanian Politics* (Danville, Ill., 1971), deals with the period 1903 to 1910. A different slant is provided by Lawrence O. Ealy, *The Republic of Panama in World Affairs, 1903–1950* (Philadelphia, 1951).

Two excellent unpublished in-house histories are Almon R. Wright, "The United States and Panama, 1933–1949," U.S. Department of State Research Project 499, 1952, and "The Department of State during the Administration of President Lyndon B. Johnson, November 1963–January 1969," Johnson Library, document 1985–2081, *Declassified Document Reference Service* (Washington, D.C., 1986).

Larry LaRae Pippin, *The Remón Era: An Analysis of a Decade of Events in Panama, 1947–1957* (Stanford, Calif., 1964), covers relations with the United States in much detail, as do Sheldon B. Liss, *The Canal: Aspects of United States–Panamanian Relations* (Notre Dame, Ind., 1967), and Steve C. Ropp, *Panamanian Politics: From Guarded Nation to National Guard* (New York, 1982), for later periods. J. Conte Porras's *Arnulfo Arias Madrid* (Panama City, 1980) is a good source for that leader's role in international affairs. George Priestley's *Military*

*Government and Popular Participation in Panama* (Boulder, Colo., 1986) treats the Torrijos regime as a populist government that suppressed the traditional elite.

The armed forces of Panama receive the closest attention from Renato Pereira, *Panamá: Fuerzas armadas e política* (Panama City, 1970), originally a doctoral dissertation. Ropp's book cited above is also good on the military. Novelist Richard M. Koster and journalist Guillermo Sánchez provide an intimate, authoritative, and provocative account of the Guardia, Torrijos, and the Noriega era with *In the Time of the Tyrants: Panama, 1968–1990* (New York, 1990).

Good accounts of the 1977 treaty story are William J. Jorden, *Panama Odyssey* (Austin, Tex., 1984); David N. Farnsworth and James W. McKenney, *U.S.-Panama Relations, 1903–1978* (Boulder, Colo., 1983); Rómulo Escobar Bethancourt, *Torrijos: Colonia americana no!* (Bogotá: 1981); J. Michael Hogan, *The Panama Canal in American Politics* (Carbondale, Ill., 1986); George D. Moffett III, *The Limits of Victory: The Ratification of the Panama Canal Treaties* (Ithaca, N.Y., 1985); and William L. Furlong and Margaret E. Scranton, *The Dynamics of Foreign Policymaking* (Boulder, Colo., 1984). An on-the-ground account is John P. Augelli's "The Panama Canal Area in Transition," American Universities Field Staff Reports, 1981, nos. 3–4.

The memoirs of statesmen also contain useful material on the 1970s, in particular Cyrus Vance's *Hard Choices* (New York, 1983), 140–57, Jimmy Carter's *Keeping Faith* (New York, 1982), 152–85, Sol M. Linowitz's *The Making of a Public Man* (Boston, 1985), chap. 7, and William Jorden's *Panama Odyssey*, cited above.

Finally, I can recommend Brittmarie Janson Pérez, "The Symbolic Duel of Power and Protest in Panama, 1968–1989," a forthcoming dissertation at the University of Texas, and Margaret Scranton, *The Noriega Years* (Boulder, Colo., 1991).

# Index